NASA

Salvatore Tocci

Watts LIBRARY™

Franklin Watts
A Division of Scholastic Inc.
New York • Toronto • London • Auckland • Sydney
Mexico City • New Delhi • Hong Kong
Danbury, Connecticut

To all who have looked to the sky and asked "Why not?"

Note to readers: Definitions for words in **bold** can be found in the Glossary at the back of this book.

Photographs © 2003: AP/Wide World Photos/NASA: 45; Corbis Images: 51 (NASA), 7 (Stocktrek), 6; Finley-Holiday Films: 41; Mark Robinson: 39; NASA: 48 (Jet Propulsion Lab Photo), 47 (Marshall/GHCC), 36 (U.S. Geological Survey, Flagstaff, Arizona), cover, 3 left, 3 right, 4, 8, 11, 12, 14, 15, 17 bottom, 18, 20, 21, 22, 24, 25, 28, 30, 31, 33, 34, 42, 46, 50; Photo Researchers, NY: 40 (Mark Marten/NASA/SS); PhotoEdit/Michael Newman: 17 top.

Library of Congress Cataloging-in-Publication Data

Tocci, Salvatore.
    NASA / by Salvatore Tocci.
        p. cm. — (Watts library)
    Summary: Examines the function of NASA and discusses its various space exploration programs and achievements.
    Includes bibliographical references and index.
    ISBN 0-531-12282-4 (lib. bdg.)   0-531-15598-6 (pbk.)
    1. United States. National Aeronautics and Space Administration—History—Juvenile literature. 2. Astronautics—United States—History—Juvenile literature. [1. United States. National Aeronautics and Space Administration. 2. Astronautics.] I. Title. II. Series.
TL793.T63 2003
629.4'0973—dc21

2003005818

Contents

Introduction
Two Disasters 5

Chapter One
Humans in Space 9

Chapter Two
Space Stations 19

Chapter Three
The Space Shuttle 29

Chapter Four
Exploring Distant Planets 37

Chapter Five
Planet Earth 43

52 **NASA—A Timeline**

54 **Glossary**

56 **To Find Out More**

59 **A Note on Sources**

61 **Index**

NASA launched the world's first weather satellite in 1960. Seen here, the satellite was known as TIROS, which is an acronym for Television Infra-Red Observation Satellite.

Two Disasters

On September 8, 1900, a powerful hurricane raged through Galveston, Texas. Just before the hurricane struck the coastal town, winds were blowing at 135 miles (217 kilometers) per hour. As the hurricane passed through Galveston, it destroyed nearly three-quarters of the town. Between 8,000 and 10,000 people were killed. The hurricane that devastated Galveston was the deadliest natural disaster in U.S. history.

On August 24, 1992, the costliest natural disaster in U.S. history struck Florida. This was Hurricane Andrew. Packing winds as strong as those that had

The hurricane that destroyed the Texas port city of Galveston on September 8, 1900, claimed more than 8,000 lives, making it the most deadly storm in U.S. history.

struck Galveston, Andrew tore across southern Florida in just four hours. The storm blew apart nearly 80,000 buildings and left almost 200,000 people homeless. Hurricane Andrew caused a record $30 billion in damage. Amazingly, only twenty-six people were killed as a direct result of the storm, mostly from flying debris and collapsing buildings.

Why did a hurricane kill so many people in Texas in 1900, when a hurricane just as powerful killed so few in 1992? Part of the answer can be found in the sky where weather satellites **orbit** Earth. A **satellite** is any object that orbits another object in space. In 1992, images from a weather satellite revealed that a major hurricane was approaching Florida. As a result, people were advised to seek shelter before Hurricane Andrew struck.

Back in 1900, the people in Texas were not as fortunate. The National Aeronautics and Space Administration (NASA) did not launch the first weather satellite until 1960. Since then, these satellites have probably helped save thousands of lives. When you think of NASA, you probably picture astronauts flying aboard the space shuttle or an unmanned

The Birth of NASA

NASA was established on July 29, 1958, when President Dwight D. Eisenhower signed the bill passed by Congress to set up the space agency. NASA began operating on October 1, 1958.

spacecraft speeding toward a distant planet. Although NASA's mission is to explore and study the universe, all of us who have never left Earth have benefited from NASA's work. Weather satellites are only part of the story.

Today, weather satellites and other imaging technology can track the progress of potentially deadly storms. Seen here is a time-lapse photograph of Hurricane Andrew approaching the Florida coast and crossing into the Gulf of Mexico.

Together, the spacecraft, lunar module, and Saturn rocket that comprised Apollo 11 towered 363 feet (111 meters) above the launch pad at what was then known as the Kennedy Space Center in Florida. These vehicles would send astronauts Neil Armstrong, Edwin "Buzz" Aldrin, and Michael Collins to the Moon.

Chapter One

Humans in Space

What do the following items have in common: cordless power tool, television satellite dish, smoke detector, and water filter? You may have answered that all these items can be found in a home, perhaps even your own. All these items also have something else in common, however. They all use technologies or materials that were originally developed by NASA to send astronauts into space.

The First Astronauts

NASA was designed as a civilian organization in charge of the United States' exploration of space. One of its first goals was to send humans into space. In 1959, NASA chose seven military pilots to be its first astronauts, a word that means "sailors of the stars." These seven men became known as the Mercury 7. Mercury, the speedy messenger of the gods in Roman mythology, was the name NASA chose for its project to send its first astronauts into space.

America, however, would not be the first nation to send an astronaut into space. The **Soviet Union** launched a man named Yuri Gagarin into space on April 12, 1961. Gagarin orbited Earth once. His successful mission was a wake-up call for NASA to send an American astronaut into space.

On May 5, 1961, NASA launched its first astronaut, Alan Shepard, from Cape Canaveral, Florida. Although NASA's success followed the Soviet Union's by only twenty-three days, the two country's space flights were very different. Gagarin had circled Earth and reached a speed of 17,544 miles (28,228

Race to the Moon

Just twenty days after Shepard's flight, President John F. Kennedy addressed Congress and said, "I believe that this nation should commit itself to achieving the goal, before the decade is out, of landing a man on the Moon and returning him safely to Earth." There was no doubt—the United States and the Soviet Union were in a race to be the first country to send astronauts safely to the Moon and back. The race would last for over eight years.

km) per hour. In contrast, Shepard traveled just 303 miles (488 km) east of Cape Canaveral and reached a speed of only 5,134 miles (8,261 km) per hour. Unlike Gagarin, however, Shepard could control the movements of his spacecraft. He could make it move up and down, side to side, and roll.

NASA first sent an astronaut into orbit around Earth on February 20, 1962, ten months after Gagarin's flight. It had taken NASA that long to build a rocket powerful enough to send an American high enough into space to enter orbit. The astronaut, John Glenn, orbited Earth three times in a flight that lasted almost five hours.

Three more Mercury flights followed Glenn's. The last one left Earth on May 15, 1963. On that flight, the astronaut, Gordon Cooper, circled Earth twenty-two times in just over thirty-four hours. Cooper became the first astronaut to sleep in space. With the success of its Mercury project, NASA showed that humans could travel safely in space for an extended period of

A specially automated camera aboard the Friendship 7 Mercury-Atlas 6 *spacecraft took this photo of astronaut John Glenn as he became the first American to orbit Earth.*

time. Now it was time for NASA to move on to the next step in landing astronauts on the Moon.

Project Gemini

To go to the Moon and back, astronauts would have to travel as a team. They would also have to leave their spacecraft and perform an **extra-vehicular activity** (**EVA**), which is commonly called a space walk. Finally, a journey to the Moon would require two spacecraft to meet and dock in space. NASA designed Project Gemini to meet all these goals. The name of this project came from the Latin word for "twins." Each spacecraft in Project Gemini carried two astronauts.

Between March 1965 and November 1966, NASA

launched ten successful Gemini flights. During the second Gemini flight, Edward White became the first American to perform an EVA. The space suit that White wore had many features designed to protect him from the conditions in space. For example, the suit had to maintain his body temperature even though the temperature in space went from 250° Fahrenheit (121° Celsius) in the sun to -150° F (-101° C) in the shade.

The next Gemini flight set a record that lasted for five years. The two astronauts aboard the spacecraft orbited Earth for almost eight days. This flight proved that astronauts could live and work in space long enough to go to the Moon and back, a round-trip that would take eight days.

After five Gemini flights, NASA had proven that it could send two astronauts into space for long periods of time. NASA had also shown that astronauts could perform EVAs. All that remained was to have two spacecraft meet and dock in space. Docking would be required to land astronauts on the Moon. While a manned spacecraft continued to orbit the Moon, a small landing craft with astronauts aboard would be sent to the lunar surface. The landing craft would then lift off from the Moon and meet up and dock with the orbiting craft for the return trip to Earth.

The first Gemini flight to dock successfully was launched on March 16, 1966. Once in orbit, the two astronauts aboard started chasing an unmanned spacecraft that had been launched hours earlier from Cape Canaveral. The astronauts succeeded in catching and docking with the other spacecraft.

UFOs

Gordon Cooper was the first astronaut in space to report seeing unidentified flying objects (UFOs).

Astronaut Harrison Schmitt explores the surface of the Moon as part of an EVA during the Apollo 17 *mission. Behind Schmitt is the lunar module (LM), which carried him to and from the Moon's surface. To his left, behind the American flag, is the LRV (lunar roving module), which Schmitt used to conduct some of the mission's EVA.*

Project Gemini had accomplished all of NASA's goals. But there was another success that came out of this project. With ten successful Gemini flights, NASA had showed that America was ready to send astronauts to the Moon. It was time for the next step.

Project Apollo

Project Apollo was NASA's final step in sending astronauts to the Moon. That final step started with a tragedy. On January 27, 1967, three astronauts boarded an Apollo spacecraft for a ground test of the equipment. A fire broke out inside the spacecraft, killing the three astronauts. Gus Grissom, Edward White, and Roger Chaffee became the first fatalities in NASA's space program.

NASA spent more than a year redesigning the Apollo spacecraft and did not launch its first manned Apollo spacecraft until October 11, 1968. The three astronauts aboard successfully orbited Earth. The Apollo spacecraft was ready to take astronauts to the Moon.

The first Apollo spacecraft to land astronauts on the Moon was launched on July 16, 1969. Neil Armstrong, Michael Collins, and Edwin Aldrin were on their way to the Moon. On July 20, the spacecraft carrying Armstrong and Aldrin landed on the Moon. The two astronauts spent about 2 1/2 hours walking on the Moon. The next day, they took off and rejoined Collins who had remained in lunar orbit. The three astronauts returned safely home to a hero's welcome.

On December 19, 1972, the last three Apollo astronauts who traveled to the Moon returned to

The effects of the fire that killed astronauts Virgil "Gus" Grissom, Edward White, and Roger Chaffee are clearly evident on the scorched exterior of the Apollo spacecraft command module.

Moon Rocket

Sending astronauts to the Moon would require the most powerful rocket ever built. NASA built the *Saturn V* for the job. The *Saturn V* was 363 feet (111 meters) tall and weighed 6 million pounds (2.7 million kilograms). The rocket had three parts, or stages, that were filled with fuel. At liftoff, the burning fuel from the first stage produced 7.7 million pounds (3.5 million kg) of thrust and set off flames that could be seen 150 miles (240 km) away. The first stage burned 2,000 tons of fuel in just 2 1/2 minutes, lifting the rocket 41 miles (66 km) above Earth.

Earth. Although it was NASA's last manned mission to the Moon, this Apollo flight marked another first for America. One of the astronauts, Harrison Schmitt, became the first scientist to travel in space. While on the Moon, Schmitt set up several experiments. He also used the cordless power tools that NASA had developed to bring back about 245 pounds (111 kg) of lunar rocks and soil samples.

NASA Spinoffs

Cordless power tools are only one of the many products used in homes today that were first developed by NASA. Such products are known as **spinoffs**, items originally developed for one purpose that are redesigned or modified for another purpose. Perhaps you have never used a cordless power tool. But you probably have used other spinoffs from NASA's projects to send astronauts to the Moon.

For example, you may use a joystick to play games on your computer. NASA developed the first joystick so that astronauts could control the vehicle they used to roam the lunar surface. You may wear sunglasses that block almost all the

The Last One

The last Apollo Moon mission took place in 1972. Since then, all human space flight has been limited to orbiting Earth.

sunlight that can damage your eyes. These glasses are a spinoff of a visor NASA developed to protect an astronaut's eyes from sunlight during an EVA. Even more spinoffs have come from the technology NASA developed to place space stations in orbit around Earth.

A boy uses a joystick to play a computer game. Few such players realize that NASA technology has been put to use in creating such games.

Reflected off the Apollo 14 *lunar module is a circular flare caused by the sun. The flare, seen by astronauts Alan Shepard and Edgar Mitchell during the mission's first EVA, was said by them to look like a jewel.*

Another type of EVA: Mission specialist Philippe Perrin works on installing systems for the Mobile Transporter, a railcar, on the International Space Station. Perrin is an astronaut for CNES, France's space agency.

Chapter Two

Space Stations

Do you play baseball? The helmet you wear at bat to protect your head may contain a foam padding that NASA first developed for astronauts' seats. Have you ever gone skiing? If you have, then the ski boots you wore are also a NASA spin-off. Ski boots are made so that skiers can flex their feet without losing any support. NASA first designed a flexible boot for astronauts to wear in space.

Baseball helmets and ski boots are just two of the many spinoffs from NASA that are now used in sports and recreation. Some of these spin-offs came from projects NASA developed to launch space stations into orbit around Earth. Space stations are places where astronauts live and work for long periods of time.

Space stations also give astronauts a good view of planets and other objects in space. Views of space from Earth are distorted by the **atmosphere**, layers of gases that surround the planet. These layers constantly shift and distort what we see of space from Earth. Being above the atmosphere gives astronauts a clearer view.

The Skylab 1 *space station orbits Earth in this photo taken by the* Skylab 2 Command and Service Module *during a routine "fly-around" inspection of the space station in June 1973.*

Skylab

The first American space station, called *Skylab*, was launched by NASA on May 14, 1973. NASA used parts salvaged from the Apollo project to build *Skylab*. The space station was 84 feet (26 m) long, weighed nearly 3 tons, and was the size of a three-bedroom house. In the first eight months after *Skylab*'s launch, NASA sent three crews of astronauts to live and work aboard the space station.

The main job of the first crew was to repair some damage that had occurred during liftoff. A shield had torn away. The shield was designed to protect *Skylab* from any meteoroid that might strike

Skylab *orbits Earth. At right on the vehicle is a solar panel. There was supposed to be a matching panel on* Skylab's *left side, but it was lost during deployment.*

it. A **meteoroid** is a small object made of rock or metal hurling through space.

The shield also served to block most of the Sun's rays to keep the temperature inside *Skylab* from getting too high. Without the shield, the temperature had risen to 126° F (52° C) inside *Skylab* when it was in the sun. On their second day in space, the astronauts fixed the problem. The crew spent twenty-eight days in space, breaking a Soviet record of twenty-three days set two years earlier. The Americans' record would not last long, however.

Space Record

The current world record for length of stay in space was set in 1994-1995 by a Russian astronaut who remained in space for 438 days.

Fellow member of the crew William R. Pogue took this photo of astronauts Jerry Carr, the mission commander (right), and Edward Gibson, the science pilot (left), at the far end of the orbital workshop aboard Skylab 4. *Also visible are three extra-vehicular mobility unit (EMU) space suits used for EVA.*

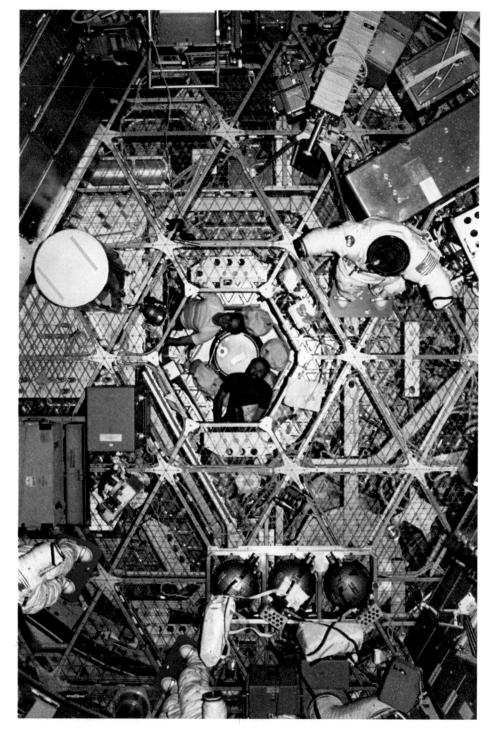

The next crew of astronauts sent to *Skylab* spent fifty-nine days in space. The third and final *Skylab* crew spent eighty-four days in space, traveling about 34 million miles (55 million km). Such long stays in space gave NASA the chance to study the effects of weightlessness on humans. An astronaut orbiting Earth is in a condition called **free fall**, the movement of an object toward Earth with little to slow the object down. While in free fall, astronauts can float inside their spacecraft. This makes them feel weightless. NASA discovered that astronauts did not experience any harmful effects from long periods of weightlessness.

NASA had hoped to keep *Skylab* in orbit until its next project was launched. To remain in orbit, *Skylab* would have to be boosted higher into space to keep it from falling back to Earth. But, NASA did not have the funds to do this. As a result, the space station fell back to Earth. On July 11, 1979, *Skylab* broke up as it reentered Earth's atmosphere and scattered in pieces over uninhabited regions of Australia and the Pacific Ocean. *Skylab* was not the only thing that had come to an end. By this time, the space competition between America and the Soviet Union had also ended.

Growing Taller

Astronauts can grow 2 inches (5 centimeters) taller while in space because of weightlessness. Because an astronaut's spine does not have to support the body's weight in space, it can stretch slightly. After returning to Earth, the astronaut's spine shrinks to its original length as it again supports the body's weight.

Working Together

Besides sending astronauts to the Moon, Project Apollo was also used to establish a working relationship between the United States and the Soviet Union in space. In 1975, an Apollo spacecraft docked with a Soviet spacecraft while in

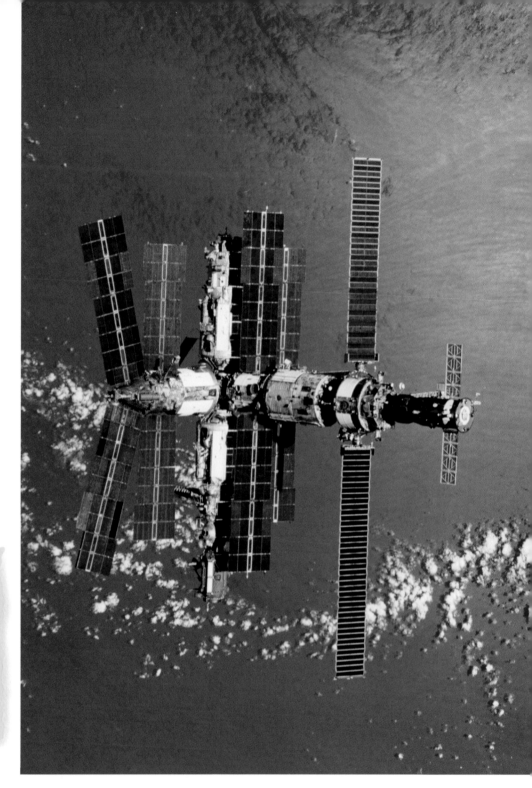

Taken from the space shuttle Atlantis, *this photograph shows Russia's space station,* Mir, *as* Atlantis *nears for docking in January 1997. The docking was to allow a U.S. astronaut aboard* Atlantis *to change places with a Russian cosmonaut aboard* Mir, *another of NASA's exercises in international cooperation in space.*

Live from Space

The first live telecast from space occurred in 1968 during the flight of *Apollo 7,* the first spacecraft to carry three American astronauts.

orbit. The astronauts were able to crawl from one spacecraft to another. When the two crews first met, they shook hands, an event that was televised live to Earth.

In 1986, the Soviet Union launched a space station called *Mir*. Seven American astronauts eventually lived aboard *Mir*, which remained in space until 1998. That same year, the first piece of the next and most ambitious space station was launched. This is the *International Space Station* (*ISS*).

Getting the *ISS* underway was no easy task. NASA originally budgeted $8 billion as its share of the cost of building the *ISS*. But this amount proved far too little. In the early 1990s, the *ISS* looked as if it would never get off the ground.

The unbearable lightness of being: Mission commander James Wetherbee, a U.S. astronaut, takes advantage of weightlessness to float about the Destiny *laboratory aboard the International Space Station.*

However, a deal between NASA and Russia was arranged. The first piece of the *ISS* was built and launched by Russia, but paid for by NASA. Today, sixteen nations are cooperating in building and operating the *ISS*.

The Biggest Thing in Orbit

Plans call for completing the *ISS* by early 2006. When finished, the *ISS* will be 290 feet (88 m) long and 360 feet (110 m) across. On Earth, the *ISS* would weigh nearly 500 tons. The size of two football fields placed side by side, the *ISS* will be the largest and heaviest object that humans have put into orbit around Earth.

The first crew boarded the *ISS* in November 2000. Like any new residents, the three astronauts—one American and two Russians—had to get used to their new living quarters. They had to wear earplugs to sleep because a machine that removed carbon dioxide from the air made a loud sound every ten minutes.

In 2001, NASA sent the Human Research Facility (HRF) to the *ISS*. The HRF was designed and built to measure changes in the astronauts' bodies during their long stays aboard the *ISS*. For example, the HRF will measure changes in an astronaut's ability to navigate. In this test, the astronaut wears a mask that is connected to a laptop computer. The mask allows the astronaut to see only what is on the computer screen. A program projects images of realistic tunnels through which the astronaut must navigate. The computer then analyzes the path the astronaut took to determine how well he or she navigated through the maze.

A Sports Spinoff

NASA has used the *ISS* to carry out experiments with various **memory metals**. These are metals that return to their original shape after they have been deliberately bent or twisted. NASA is experimenting with memory metals to find out if they are suitable for making airplane wings. Such wings would be flexible, allowing an airplane to perform maneuvers that are not possible now.

A memory metal developed by NASA is used to build the heads on some golf clubs. As the head strikes the golf ball, the metal changes shape. This change in shape keeps the club and ball in contact longer. As a result, the golf ball has more spin as it travels through the air. The extra spin causes the ball to stop more quickly when it hits the putting green. Many golfers may be able to improve their scores, thanks to this NASA spinoff. Another NASA project has led to even more spinoffs. This is the space shuttle.

Riding the back of a booster rocket, the space shuttle Endeavour *lifts off on June 5, 2002.* Endeavour's *destination on that mission was the* International Space Station. *Despite the* Challenger *and* Columbia *tragedies, the space shuttle is one of NASA's proudest achievements. It is the first craft capable of returning on its own to Earth.*

The Space Shuttle

Like most young people, you probably like to play outdoors when the weather is nice. Unfortunately, some young people must be very careful whenever they go outdoors on a sunny day. These children suffer from a very rare medical condition—they do not have any sweat glands. Sweating is the body's way of keeping cool. Without sweat glands, these children can suffer heatstroke and even die by playing outdoors on a sunny day.

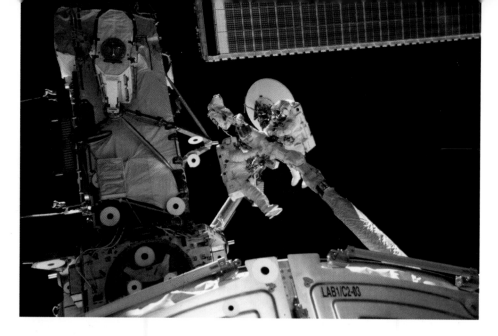

Those who have conducted EVA outside the space shuttle, like astronauts Linda Godwin (lower left) and Daniel Tani, seen here working on Endeavour, *report that it is one of the most exhilirating experiences imaginable.*

Fortunately, these children can now play outdoors whenever they want, thanks to NASA. All they have to do is wear a "cool suit." This suit is made of a special layer of clothing lined with plastic pouches that are filled with a waxy solid.

Outdoors, the waxy solid absorbs the heat from the Sun and slowly melts inside the pouches. By absorbing heat, the solid in the pouches keeps the child's body from overheating. The cool suit can be reused by placing the pouches in a refrigerator to turn the melted wax back into a solid. This cool suit is a spinoff of a space suit that NASA designed for astronauts to wear during their EVAs aboard the space shuttle.

A Reusable Spacecraft

Unlike the reusable cool suit, the spacecraft NASA launched in its Mercury, Gemini, and Apollo projects were good for only one use. Some of these spacecraft later made a trip to a museum. Not one, however, made another trip into space.

Building a new spacecraft for each launch cost a lot of money.

In the 1970s, NASA realized that future space missions would have to cost much less. One way to save money was to develop a spacecraft that could be reused as often as needed. In addition, NASA wanted to build a spacecraft that could deliver cargo into space. In this way, companies that wanted to launch their own satellites would help pay the cost of space missions. NASA's solution was to build the Space Transportation System, which is the space shuttle's official name. Although it is not completely reusable, the space shuttle has accomplished NASA's goal of saving money.

NASA launched the first shuttle, named *Columbia*, on April 12, 1981, from Cape Canaveral. Like all spacecraft launched by NASA, the shuttle travels into space aboard a rocket. But unlike earlier spacecraft, the shuttle returns from space like a plane.

The shuttle *Columbia* made five

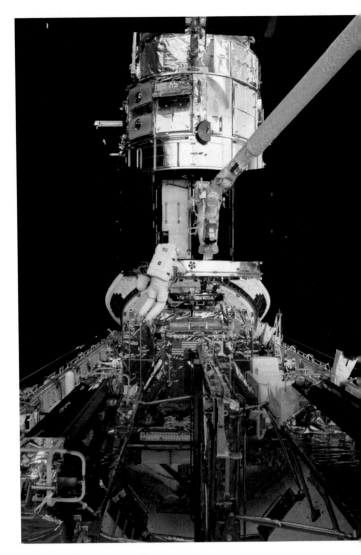

NASA has so expanded the capabilities of space flight that repair missions, such as this March 2002 flight by the space shuttle Columbia *to provide maintenance on the* Hubble Space Telescope, *have come to seem almost routine. Astronauts James Newman and Michael Massimino can be seen here using* Columbia's *remote manipular arm to replace one of Hubble's cameras.*

successful trips in space. One goal of these missions was to test a robot arm. This device is used to remove cargo from the shuttle and place it in space. For its sixth shuttle mission, NASA launched its new shuttle named *Challenger*. Sally K. Ride became America's first woman astronaut on *Challenger's* second shuttle mission that was launched on June 18, 1983. The next *Challenger* flight, launched on August 30, 1983, brought another first: Guion S. Bluford became the first African-American in space.

The *Challenger* and *Columbia* Tragedies

Americans soon got used to a shuttle being launched into space on a regular basis. By the beginning of 1986, NASA had launched twenty-four successful shuttle missions. Then, on January 28, 1986, the second human tragedy in NASA's space program occurred. That morning, the shuttle *Challenger* again blasted off into space. Seven astronauts were aboard, including S. Christa McAuliffe, the first teacher to travel into space. Just seventy-three seconds after liftoff, *Challenger* blew up. All seven astronauts were killed.

NASA suspended future shuttle launches while it investigated the cause of the *Challenger* disaster. NASA discovered that a leaky seal allowed a booster rocket to break loose and drag *Challenger* out of control. Not until September 29, 1988, did NASA again launch a shuttle. After orbiting Earth for four days, *Discovery*, which had been redesigned, returned safely

The Space Shuttle

A space shuttle consists of three parts. One part is the orbiter, where the astronauts live and work. Two huge rocket boosters that lift the shuttle into orbit make up the second part. The third part is a large fuel tank that supplies the orbiter's three main engines. The fuel tank is the only part that is not reused. When all three parts are assembled and fueled, a space shuttle is about 184 feet (56 m) tall and weighs about 2,250 tons.

home. NASA was back in business with the space shuttle. However, another tragedy struck the space shuttle program on February 1, 2003.

On the way home after a sixteen-day mission, the space shuttle *Columbia* broke apart shortly after reentering Earth's atmosphere. The shuttle was traveling at about 12,500 miles (20,000 km) per hour some 38 miles (61 km) above land when the tragedy occurred. Investigators discovered that super-heated gases may have penetrated the space shuttle through damaged surface tiles on its left wing. These gases then caused

Columbia to break apart. The seven astronauts aboard, including six Americans and the first Israeli in space, were killed.

Eye in the Sky

When the shuttle *Discovery* took off in April 1990, attention was focused not on the astronauts, but on the cargo that was aboard. The shuttle was carrying the *Hubble Space Telescope* (*HST*). The astronauts aboard used the shuttle's robot arm to remove the *HST* from the cargo bay and place it in orbit about 370 miles (595 km) above Earth. Equipped with cutting-edge technology, the *HST* was designed to take a close look into deep space.

The *HST* has provided the closest and clearest look at distant planets, such as Uranus, Neptune, and Pluto. The *HST* has also taken images of galaxies so far away that it has in effect looked back some 11 billion years, at a time when the universe was young. But the images that the *HST* is now providing were not always clear. When it was first put into orbit in 1990, the *HST* could not focus properly. In 1993, NASA launched its sixty-first shuttle mission. The main job of the astronauts aboard was to fix the problem with the *HST*.

Since that successful repair, NASA has launched three more shuttle missions to update the *HST*. The latest was the shuttle *Columbia*, launched on March 1, 2002. During their EVAs, the astronauts installed some 6,000 pounds (2,700 kg) of equipment on the *HST*. One item was a camera that is about the size of a telephone booth.

Shuttle Service

The last shuttle to service the *HST* is scheduled for launch in 2004. This should enable the space telescope to complete its twenty-year mission in 2010.

The great canyon known as Valle Marineris is clearly visible as it cuts across the surface of Mars in this NASA image. The dark, reddish spots near the top of the planet are the three giant volcanoes of Tharsis.

Chapter Four

Exploring Distant Planets

Have you ever had your temperature taken by a thermometer that was put in your ear? The thermometer detects heat given off by the eardrum. A tiny computer chip converts this heat to a temperature that is displayed digitally. Some ear thermometers do this in two seconds or less. The ear thermometer is a spinoff of a device NASA installed on its spacecraft to measure the temperature of distant planets.

NASA's First Launch

The first NASA project designed to explore the solar system beyond Earth was called Pioneer. The first satellite ever launched by NASA was appropriately called *Pioneer 1*. The launch took place on October 11, 1958, less than three months after NASA had been established. NASA planned to send *Pioneer 1* into orbit around the Moon. But, the satellite traveled only about 70,789 miles (113,854 km), or about one-quarter of the distance to the Moon.

NASA launched a total of thirteen Pioneer satellites over a period of twenty years. Launched in 1972, *Pioneer 10* flew by Jupiter and then became the first human-made object ever to leave our solar system. In 1979, *Pioneer 11* flew within 13,000 miles (20,900 km) of Saturn.

In the late 1970s, *Pioneer 12* and *Pioneer 13* orbited Venus and mapped the planet's surface. *Pioneer 13* also sent four probes through the Venusian atmosphere. One landed on the surface of Venus and sent signals back to Earth for more than an hour before its batteries drained. With the success of its Pioneer project, NASA had probed into the far reaches of space. But it was just the beginning of what NASA would find out about the solar system.

First in Space

The United States launched its first satellite, *Explorer 1*, into orbit around Earth on January 31, 1958. The Soviet Union had launched a satellite called *Sputnik 1* into orbit almost four months earlier.

Studying the Solar System

The list of spacecraft that NASA has launched to study the solar system is long. Since *Pioneer 4* became NASA's first spacecraft to travel outside Earth's orbit on its way to the

Moon in 1959, spacecraft have orbited or flown by all the planets except Pluto. The information that these spacecraft have collected has filled many books. What follows are only a few of the many interesting discoveries that NASA spacecraft have made about our solar system, starting with the Sun.

The spacecraft *SOHO* detected steady wind speeds on the Sun that reach 198,800 miles per hour (320,000 km per hour). At this speed, winds would take less than a minute to cross the Atlantic Ocean.

Mercury has been visited by only one spacecraft, *Mariner 10*, which found an extreme range of temperatures on the planet. Mercury has almost the highest temperatures of any planet in the solar system and almost the coldest temperatures.

Venus is surrounded by dense clouds that made it impossible to see its surface until the spacecraft *Magellan* arrived.

Visiting Pluto

NASA hopes to launch a spacecraft in early 2006 that will arrive at Pluto some time between 2015 and 2017.

Mariner 10 *provided this image of the surface of the planet Mercury. Scientists speculate that the light blue areas in the image may be ancient volcanoes.*

This computer-generated representation of the surface of the planet Venus is based on data collected by Magellan. The image shows three craters—Howe, Danilova, and Aglaonice— in the northwest region of Lavinia Planitia in Venus's southern hemisphere.

Using radar, *Magellan* mapped more than 98 percent of the planet's surface and revealed that it is covered with volcanic material, such as lava.

Mars became the first planet after Earth to have a human-made object orbit it. While orbiting Mars, *Mariner 9* discovered the largest known volcano in the solar system. Named Olympus Mons, this volcano is 17 miles (27 km) high and 373 miles (600 km) wide.

The spacecraft *Galileo* dropped a probe into Jupiter's atmosphere, which sent back important information about its composition.

Saturn has been visited by two *Voyager* spacecraft. The planet is surrounded by an enormous system of rings. These rings are so large that they would extend from the Earth to the Moon. The *Voyager* spacecraft discovered that Saturn's rings are made mostly of ice.

When *Voyager 2* visited Uranus, it discovered ten more moons orbiting the planet. Uranus is now known to have twenty-one moons.

Neptune was also photographed by *Voyager 2*. The spacecraft discovered six new moons and three new rings that orbit the planet.

This color-enhanced view of Mars shows dark patches on the planet's surface. The image was sent back to Earth by the Mars Global Surveyor.

Back on Earth

The technologies that NASA developed to explore our solar system have led to spinoffs now used for health care. Ear thermometers are just one example. Another such spinoff is a vision screening system for children. A digital camera takes images of a child's eyes. In less than one minute, a computer analyzes the images for various vision problems. During the early 1990s, about 50,000 American children were screened using this system. About 4,000 were given immediate medical attention to prevent them from developing permanent vision problems.

Straight Teeth

Clear braces that are almost invisible are another NASA spinoff.

Although NASA's mission is space, much of its work has applications back here on Earth. This photo, taken from the space shuttle Atlantis in January 1997, shows the delta of the Nile River, in Egypt, with the huge city of Cairo on the east (right) bank.

Chapter Five

Planet Earth

People use many NASA spinoffs in their daily lives. These spinoffs are considered *indirect* benefits of NASA's work because they are based on technologies that NASA first developed for their space program. For example, NASA developed rechargeable, long-life batteries to power the instruments on spacecraft. These batteries led to the rechargeable batteries that are used to power devices that we use every day.

But people have also benefited *directly* from NASA programs. For example, weather satellites provide continuous information about our global climate.

Their warnings about approaching storms, such as the hurricane that struck Florida in 1992, have saved many lives. These satellites have also warned us of an even more serious threat to planet Earth.

The Ozone Layer

In the 1980s, a weather satellite, *Nimbus* 7, confirmed that a problem had developed with the ozone layer. **Ozone** is a chemical produced when sunlight strikes oxygen in the air. Ozone forms a thin layer that surrounds Earth about 12 to 30 miles (19 to 48 km) above sea level.

The ozone layer blocks most of the Sun's ultraviolet light from reaching Earth. If more ultraviolet light did reach Earth, it would damage plant and animal life and cause a large increase in the number of people with skin cancer. Images provided by *Nimbus* 7 showed that a huge hole had formed in the ozone layer. This hole, which appears over Antarctica for several months every year, is growing bigger. In 2000, the hole measured about 11 million square miles (28 million square km), larger than the entire North American continent.

Scientists concluded that the hole was caused by chemicals used in aerosol sprays, refrigerators, and air-conditioning systems. These chemicals slowly drift to the upper atmosphere where they break apart the ozone. The images provided by NASA weather satellites helped convince countries to ban the use of these chemicals. Scientists hope that the ozone layer will be able to repair itself.

Rather Thin

The ozone layer is only the thickness of two stacked pennies.

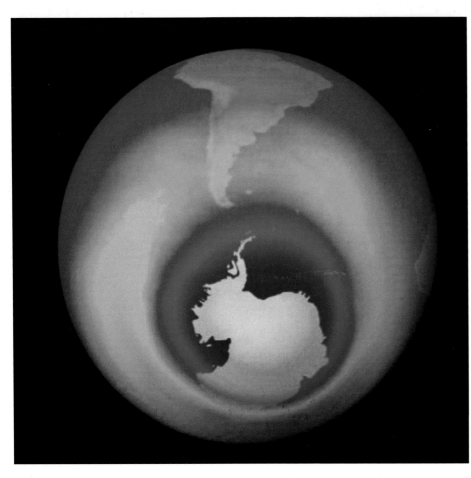

NASA's TOMS (Total Ozone Mapping Spectrometer) Earth Probe shows clearly, in blue, the depletion of the ozone layer over Antarctica. Damage to the ozone layer is a primary cause of global warming.

Watching over Earth

Partly because of what *Nimbus 7* had discovered, NASA began a program in 1991 to study Earth much more closely than it had. NASA calls its new program Earth Science Enterprise. For this program, spacecraft were not launched to some distant part of the solar system, but rather sent into orbit around Earth.

Cameras and other instruments onboard spacecraft in orbit provide close-up images and other information about our

View from Space

The process of taking close-up images of Earth from space is called remote sensing.

Taken with a handheld camera through a window of the space shuttle Atlantis, *this photograph shows the great commercial city-state of Singapore, on the Malay peninsula in southeast Asia. Images such as this one can be used to study the effects of urbanization on the land and environment over time.*

NASA and Farming

NASA uses cameras to photograph farmers' fields. These cameras photograph not only what the human eye *can* see but also what it *cannot* see. Images are taken of a field as it appears in visible light, which we can see, and also in infrared light, which we cannot see.

Healthy plants reflect infrared light well. But plants that are wilted or infected with insects do not reflect infrared light as well. As a result, plants that need attention appear darker in images taken with infrared light.

These images are sent to the farmer in as little as twenty-four hours. A farmer can then attend to the problem before any serious damage is done.

planet's land, water, and air. These images and information are used in making plans to control damage from disasters, such as wildfires and floods, and to manage resources, such as forests and farmlands.

To see how NASA helps farmers plan, consider Neal Isbell whose family has been growing crops in northern Alabama for six generations. Isbell is one of a new generation of farmers who practice "precision agriculture." These farmers use information provided by NASA satellites and planes to determine which areas in their fields need fertilizer, water, or weed control. As a result, these farmers do not have to waste time

One practical application on Earth of NASA observation technology is in the field known as precision agriculture. Data collected by the ATLAS remote sensing instrument aboard a NASA airplane is used to create an image, such as this one, of a particular plot of land. Trained observers can use the image to obtain information about such things as the content and health of soil, availability of water, evaporation, and overall suitability for agriculture.

tending to crops that do not require care. These farmers also save money, especially by not using fertilizers where they are not needed. With 4,200 acres (1,700 hectares) of cotton to care for, Isbell has saved a lot of time and money.

Uncovering the Past

Images taken by NASA satellites and planes have also uncovered information about Earth's past. In 1981, images from a space shuttle discovered the lost city of Ubar in the Sahara Desert in Africa. Instruments aboard the shuttle recorded images of a network of tracks that helped pinpoint the city, which lay buried beneath the desert sand. NASA

NASA imaging technology can even be used to gain knowledge about human history. This radar image obtained by the space shuttle Endeavour *in April 1994 was used to determine the location of the lost city of Ubar, a remote desert trading outpost in what is now the nation of Oman on the Arabian peninsula. Ubar vanished from recorded history in about the year 300, but this image revealed ancient tracks (thin reddish streaks near center) leading to and from the lost trade center.*

images also revealed that the Sahara, the driest place on Earth, once had rivers and lakes.

Images taken from a shuttle also revealed a hidden section of the ancient city of Angkor in Cambodia. During the ninth century, the city was home to more than one million people. Today, much of it is covered by a thick jungle. NASA images detected canals north of the main city that cannot be seen from the ground. Scientists now believe that Angkor was even larger than they had once thought.

Extraterrestrial Life

In 2002, NASA asked about 100 scientists to meet and discuss one issue: Does extraterrestrial life exist? In other words, does life exist someplace in the universe other than Earth? This is an appropriate question for NASA to explore. After all, NASA has launched dozens of missions to study our solar system and to peer into the far reaches of our universe. NASA has also launched spacecraft to take a close look at Earth, including its life-forms. So it's logical for NASA to explore whether life, which is found everywhere on Earth, exists anywhere else in our universe.

The search for extraterrestrial life has led to a new branch of science called **astrobiology**, which is the study of the origin, evolution, and distribution of life in the universe. To find life as we know it elsewhere in the universe, scientists must first find an Earth-like planet. Earth is a **terrestrial planet**, one made of solid materials like rocks and metals. In addition

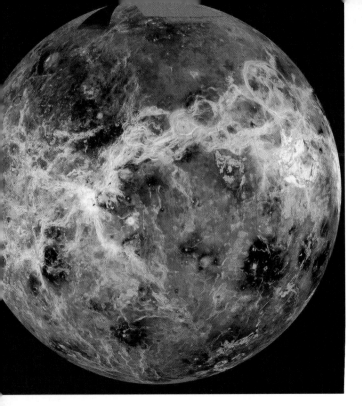

Data provided by Venera 13 and 14, Magellan, and Pioneer was used to create this image of Venus, showing the topography of the planet.

to Earth, the terrestrial planets in our solar system are Mercury, Venus, Mars, and Pluto. Jupiter, Saturn, Neptune, and Uranus are known as **gas giants**, because they are huge balls of gases and liquids.

Telescopes on Earth have so far found more than a hundred planets orbiting nearby stars. However, all of these planets are gas giants, where life is not likely to exist. Over the next two decades, NASA will launch several missions to search a part of the Milky Way galaxy for terrestrial planets. One, called the *Kepler* mission, is scheduled for launch in 2007. The satellite, which will be placed into orbit around the Sun, will study 100,000 other distant stars, looking for terrestrial planets.

Finding a terrestrial planet orbiting a distant star is no easy task. The planet must pass in front of the star as seen from Earth and block enough of the star's light for scientists to determine if it is a terrestrial planet. NASA scientists have compared what they must do to the challenge of finding an ant crawling across the headlight of one car miles away on a highway filled with cars, all with their headlights on. This challenge may seem impossible. However, the challenge of sending astronauts to the Moon also seemed impossible at one time. NASA proved it could be done.

Astronaut Alan Shepard plants the U.S. flag on the Moon. Putting a man on the moon is one of NASA's greatest accomplishments; it is a feat that no other country has come close to duplicating.

NASA—A Timeline

1957	The Soviet Union launches the first artificial satellite, *Sputnik 1*.
1958	The United States launches its first satellite, *Explorer 1*. (January) The law establishing NASA is signed. (July) NASA launches *Pioneer 1*. (October)
1959	NASA launches *Pioneer 4* to the Moon. (March) NASA selects its first seven astronauts, known as the Mercury 7. (April)
1960	NASA launches the first weather satellite, *TIROS 1*, and the first communications satellite, *Echo 1*.
1961	Alan Shepard becomes America's first astronaut in space.
1962	John Glenn becomes the first American to orbit Earth.
1965	NASA launches its first manned Gemini mission. (March) Edward White becomes the first American to walk in space. (June)
1966	NASA lands an unmanned spacecraft on the Moon.
1967	Three astronauts are killed in a fire while performing a ground test of an Apollo spacecraft.
1968	NASA launches its first successful manned Apollo mission.
1969	Two Apollo astronauts, Neil Armstrong and Edwin Aldrin, walk on the Moon.
1972	The last Apollo mission returns from the Moon.
1973	NASA launches *Skylab*. (May) NASA sends its first unmanned mission to fly by two planets, Venus and Mercury. (November)
1977	*Voyager 1* and *Voyager 2* are launched to study the giant gas planets.

1981	NASA launches its first space shuttle.
1983	Sally K. Ride becomes the first American woman in space. Guion S. Bluford becomes the first African American in space.
1986	Seven astronauts are killed when the shuttle *Challenger* explodes shortly after launch.
1990	The *Hubble Space Telescope* is placed in orbit around Earth.
1998	NASA begins construction of the *International Space Station*, which is scheduled for completion in 2006.
2002	NASA gathers scientists to plan missions to look for extraterrestrial life.
2003	Seven astronauts are killed when the space shuttle *Columbia* breaks apart while returning to Earth.

Glossary

astrobiology—the study of the origin, evolution, and distribution of life in the universe

atmosphere—the layers of gases that surround a planet

extra-vehicular activity (EVA)—an activity performed in space by an astronaut outside a spacecraft; commonly referred to as a space walk

free fall—the movement of an object toward Earth with little to slow it down

gas giant—a planet such as Jupiter that is a huge ball of gases and liquids

memory metal—a metal that returns to its original shape after it has been deliberately bent or twisted

meteoroid—a small object made of rock or metal hurling through space

orbit—to travel around a particular object in space; the path an object takes as it travels around another object in space

ozone—a chemical that forms a layer above Earth that protects against the Sun's ultraviolet light

satellite—any object that orbits another object in space. Earth is a natural satellite of the Sun. The *Hubble Space Telescope* is an artificial satellite, or one made by humans, of Earth.

Soviet Union—a nation formed in 1922 when Russia combined with other countries in eastern Europe and central Asia. It broke apart in 1991.

spinoff—an object or device that was originally designed for some other use

terrestrial planet—a planet such as Earth that is made of solid materials like rocks and metals

To Find Out More

Books

Baker, David. Scientific American *Inventions from Outer Space: Everyday Uses for NASA Technology*. New York: Random House, 2000.

Bredeson, Carmen. *NASA Planetary Spacecraft*. Berkeley Heights, NJ: Enslow, 2000.

Campbell, Ann-Jeanette. *The New York Public Library's Amazing Space: A Book of Answers for Kids*. New York: Wiley, 1997.

Cole, Michael D. *NASA Space Vehicles*. Berkeley Heights, NJ: Enslow, 2000.

Jones, Thomas D., and Michael Benson. *The Complete Idiot's Guide to NASA*. Indianapolis, IN: Alpha Books, 2002.

Mullane, R. Mike. *Do Your Ears Pop in Space?: And 500 Surprising Questions about Space Travel*. New York: Wiley, 1997.

Spangenburg, Ray, and Kit Moser. *The History of NASA*. Danbury, CT: Franklin Watts, 2000.

Organizations and Online Sites

NASA Space Camp
http://www.spacecamp.com/spacecamp/
Find out how you can train like an astronaut. NASA operates two Space Camps in the United States for kids ages nine and older. This site has information about the program, including the dates and prices.

NASA Visitors Center and Tours
http://www.nasa.gov/about/visiting/
You can get information about the National Air and Space Museum in Washington, D.C., where you can see a collection of spacecraft used in NASA missions. This site also lists NASA centers located throughout the United States where visitors are welcome. One such center is the Kennedy Space Center in Cape Canaveral, Florida, where you can see a space shuttle launch.

National Aeronautics and Space Administration
Headquarters Information Center
Washington, D.C. 20546-0001
http://www.hq.nasa.gov/office/hqlibrary/ic/nasaic.htm
info-center@hq.nasa.gov
The NASA Information Center provides information brochures, mission decals, and posters for free and also sells various publications.

National Aeronautics and Space Administration
http://www.nasa.gov
The NASA home page includes NASA for Kids, Webcasts that are available for downloading, and updated information about the *International Space Station*.

National Space Society
600 Pennsylvania Avenue, S.E.
Suite 201
Washington, D.C. 20003
http://www.nss.org
Click on "Education" to get information about *The Space Educator*, a free publication.

A Note on Sources

My first step in writing this book was to get an overall view of what NASA has done since it started operating in 1958. I quickly learned that plenty of information exists. Many books have been written about each project that NASA has undertaken. Trying to sort through all this information would have taken a long time.

I soon realized that I needed to find a source that provided an overview of what NASA has done. In this way, I could select certain missions to focus on and then search other sources for additional details. Because there are so many names, dates, and places involved, I also wanted to be sure that my basic source was up-to-date and reliable. Ideally, it would be written by someone who could provide a first-hand account of some of NASA's projects and have direct access to information about its other projects. *The Complete Idiot's Guide to NASA*, which was written by former astronaut Thomas D. Jones and

Michael Benson, became the starting point for each chapter in this book. Dr. Jones has flown on three of the four space shuttles in operation today.

Another up-to-date and reliable source of information was NASA itself. Finding the right people at NASA, sending them my questions, and then waiting for their responses would be time-consuming. So I decided to check out NASA on the Internet. Using a search engine, I typed in certain keywords. For example, the keywords "NASA" and "astrobiology" gave me the information I used to write about the space agency's mission to search for extraterrestrial life. The keywords "NASA" and "spinoffs" led me to all sorts of everyday devices that were developed by the space agency. I owe a special thanks to NASA for posting so much information about their missions on the Internet.

Index

Numbers in *italics* indicate illustrations.

Aldrin, Edwin, 15
Apollo program, 14–16, *17*, 23
Armstrong, Neil, 15
Astrobiology, 49
Astronauts, 9–17, *18*, 20, 21, 23, 24–25, 26, 32. *See also specific names*
Atmosphere, 20, 23, 34, 38, 40

Bluford, Guion S., 32

Cape Canaveral, 11, 13
Carr, Jerry, *22*
Chaffee, Roger, 14, *15*
Challenger, *28*, 32
CNES, *18*
Collins, Michael, 15

Columbia, *28*, 31, 34–35
Cooper, Gordon, 11, 13

Discovery, 32, *33*

Earth images, *42*, *46*. *47–48*
Earth Science Enterprise, 45
Eisenhower, Dwight D., 7
Endeavour, *29*, *30*, *48*
Extra-vehicular activity (EVA), 12, 13, *14*, 22, 30, *30*, 35
Extra-vehicular mobility unit (EMU), *22*

Farming, 46, 47
Free fall, 23

Gagarin, Yuri, 10

Galileo, 40
Gas giant, 50
Gemini program, 12–14
Gibson, Edward, *22*
Glenn, John, 11, *12*
Godwin, Linda, 30
Grissom, Gus, 14, *15*

Hubble Space Telescope (HST),
  31, 35
Human Research Facility
  (HRF), 26
Hurricane Andrew, 5–6, 7

International Space Station
  (ISS), *18*, 25–27
Isbell, Neal, 47–48

Joystick, 16, *17*
Jupiter, 38, 40, 50

Kennedy, John F., 10–11, *11*
Kennedy Space Center, *8*
Kepler mission, 50

Lunar roving module (LRV),
  14

Magellan, 39–40, *41*
Mariner 10, 39, *39*, 40

Mars, *36*, 40, *41*, 50
Massimino, Michael, *31*
McAuliffe, S. Christa, 32
Memory metal, 27
Mercury, 39, 50
Mercury program, 10–11, *12*
Meteoroid, 20, 21
Mir, *24*, 25
Mitchell, Edgar, *17*
Mobile Transporter, *18*
Moon missions, 12–16

Neptune, 50
Newman, James, *31*

Orbit, 6, 11, 15, 16, 20, *21*,
  26, 38, 45, 50
Ozone, 44

Perrin, Philippe, *18*
Pioneer, 38
Pluto, 39, 50
Pogue, William R., *22*
Precision agriculture, 47–48

Remote sensing, 45
Ride, Sally K., 32

Satellite, *4*, 6, 7, 38. *See also*
  Weather satellite

Saturn, 38, 50
Saturn V, 16
Schmitt, Harrison, *14*, 16
Shepard, Alan, 10–11, *17*, *51*
Skylab, 20–23
SOHO, 39
Soviet Union, 10, 23, 25–26
Space shuttle, *28*, 29–38, *33*, *34*, 48
Space station, *18*, 19–23
Space Transportation System, 31. *See also* Space shuttle
Spinoff, 16, 19–20, 27, 30, 37, 41, 43
Sputnik I, 38

Tani, Daniel, 30
Telecast, 24

Terrestrial planet, 49–50
Television Infra-Red Observation Satellite (TIROS), *4*
Total Ozone Mapping Spectrometer (TOMS), *45*

Unidentified flying objects (UFOs), 13
Uranus, 41, 50

Venus, 38, 39, *40*, 50, *50*

Weather satellite, *4*, 7, 43–44
Weightlessness, 23
Wetherbee, James, 25
White, Ed, 13, 14, *15*

About the Author

Salvatore Tocci taught high school and college science for almost thirty years. He has a bachelor's degree from Cornell University and a master's degree from the City University of New York.

He has written books that deal with a range of science topics, from biographies of famous scientists to a high school chemistry text. He has also presented workshops at national science conventions showing teachers how to emphasize the applications of scientific knowledge in our everyday lives.

Tocci lives in East Hampton, New York, with his wife, Patti. Both retired from teaching, they spend their leisure time sailing and traveling. On a recent trip to Florida, they went to Cape Canaveral to see a shuttle launch. Unfortunately, it was postponed.

ED McBAIN

Cop Hater

POCKET BOOKS
New York London Toronto Sydney Singapore

This book is a work of fiction. Names, characters, places and in-
cidents are products of the author's imagination or are used fic-
titiously. Any resemblance to actual events or locales or persons,
living or dead, is entirely coincidental.

POCKET BOOKS, a division of Simon & Schuster Inc.
1230 Avenue of the Americas, New York, NY 10020

Copyright © 1956 by Ed McBain
Copyright renewed © 1984 by Evan Hunter
Introduction copyright © 1989 by Ed McBain

Published by arrangement with the Author

ISBN: 0-671-77547-2

First Pocket Books printing December 1999

10 9 8 7 6 5 4 3 2 1

POCKET and colophon are registered trademarks of
Simon & Schuster Inc.

Cover design by Tony Palladino
Front cover photo by Ed Holub/Photonica

Printed in the U.S.A.

This new edition of the very first
87th Precinct novel is dedicated to
my dearest darling wife—

DRAGICA DIMITRIJEVIĆ-HUNTER

INTRODUCTION

Cop Hater, the first of the 87th Precinct novels, was originally published in paperback early in 1956.

My records indicate that I received payment for the book on January 4, 1956, which would further seem to indicate that it was delivered sometime in December of 1955. I don't remember how long it took to write. The early McBains usually took a month. Nowadays, perhaps because the novels are longer, they take *two* months. *Cop Hater* took a much longer time because there was a lot of research to do for the first book in the series. I still do research, of course, but not as much as I had to do when I was initially figuring out police procedures and routines. In any case, the actual writing time is vague in my memory. I didn't keep work calendars then, as I do now.

What is *not* vague is the genesis of the series.

I had written a great many mystery short stories and a few mystery novels before *The Blackboard Jungle* was published in October of 1954. Some of these stories were published under my own name (Evan

Hunter), others under various pseudonyms. I would often have two or three stories in the same issue of a magazine like *Manhunt*, for example, all under different pseudonyms. One mystery novel written under a pseudonym had not yet sold by the time *The Blackboard Jungle* was published, and my agent was still shopping it around in 1955. Pocket Books, Inc. was at the time, publishing a handful of paperback originals in its Permabooks line, so my agent sent this novel (I believe it was *Runaway Black* as by Richard Marsten, but I'm not sure) to Herbert Alexander, then editor-in-chief of Pocket Books, Inc. and a man who was instrumental in purchasing reprint rights to *The Blackboard Jungle*.

He was possibly the smartest man who ever lived.

He was also a good detective.

He finished reading the pseudonymous mystery novel, called my agent immediately, and asked, "Is this our friend Hunter?" When he learned that the true author was *indeed* Hunter, he said he would like to have a meeting with me. (The Hollywood term "take a meeting" had not yet been invented, and anyway this was New York.)

Over lunch, Herb told me that the mainstay of Pocket Books was Erle Stanley Gardner, whose books they reissued on a regular rotating schedule, with new covers on them each time out. He told me that Gardner was getting old (I don't know how old he was in 1955) and that they were looking for a mystery writer who would eventually replace him. Herb hadn't much liked the pseudonymous novel (he didn't *buy* it, did he?) but he recognized from it that I was familiar with the form, and if I had an idea for a mystery series with a fresh and original lead character, then I was the man for them. I said I didn't have an idea in my head, but that I would like some time to think about it. We promised we'd stay in touch.

The mystery stories I'd written up to that point were a mixed bag. Private Eye, Woman in Jeopardy, Innocent Bystander, Man on the Run, Biter Bit, *and* several police stories. The novels, if I recall, were either Innocent Bystander or Man on the Run. I had most enjoyed writing the police stories which were frankly influenced by the old *Dragnet* series on radio and it seemed to me that a good series character would be a cop, even though I knew next to nothing about cops at the time. I knew for certain that any *other* character dealing with murder was unconvincing. If you came home late at night and found your wife murdered in the bed you shared, you didn't call a private eye, and you didn't call a little old lady with knitting needles, and if you called your lawyer it was to ask what you should say when you called the police. In fiction, there is always a quantum jump to be made when anyone but a police detective is investigating a murder. I come up against it in my Matthew Hope series. Hope is a lawyer who has no right investigating murders. Disbelief must be overcome, first by the author himself, and then by the reader. This isn't the case with a police detective. He is *supposed* to investigate murders.

So, yes, a cop.

But then, thinking it through further, it seemed to me that a single cop did not a series make, and it further seemed to me that something new in the annals of police procedurals (I don't even know if they were called that back then) would be a squad room *full* of cops, each with different traits, who when put together would form a *conglomerate* hero. There had been police novels before I began the 87th Precinct series. There had not, to my knowledge, been any to utilize such a concept. I felt, at the time, that it was unique. So, then, a squad room of police detectives as my conglomerate hero. And, of course, New York City as the setting.

I called Herb Alexander. I told him that I wanted to use a *lot* of cops as my hero, one cop stepping forward in one novel, another in the next novel, cops getting killed and disappearing from the series, other cops coming in, all of them visible to varying extents in each of the books. He said he liked the idea, and would give me a contract for three novels—"to see how it goes."

I began my research.

I found that the New York City Police Department was somewhat reluctant to let the author of *The Blackboard Jungle* into its precincts or its cars. Perhaps they felt I was about to do a number on them. A contact told me I could gain access by paying off a judge, a captain, and God knew how many sergeants. I told him that wasn't the kind of access I wanted. Finally, and after much perseverance, I was allowed to visit and take notes, except when prisoners were being interrogated. I rode with cops, I talked with cops, I spent hours in squad rooms and labs and at line-ups (now defunct except for identification purposes), and in court, and in holding cells until I felt I knew what being a cop was all about. And then, promising every cop I met that I would undoubtedly be calling him for further information once I got into the first book, I sat down to write.

And discovered that I was calling the NYPD almost daily. As gracious as they were, I soon learned that cops had real crimes to solve, lab technicians were often too busy to discuss my problems at length, forensics specialists had open corpses on the table at the moment and could not be bothered with fictitious ones. I learned, in short, that I was becoming a pain in the neck. And I realized early on that if I had to count on the NYPD to verify every detail of the procedure in the books I was writing, I would have to spend more time on the phone than I was spending at the typewriter.

So I asked myself why I had to use a *real* city?

What if the city I used was *like* New York, but not *quite* New York. What if I premised my geography only loosely on the real city, stuck with routine that was realistic for any police department in America ("clinical verity," Herb later called it), and then winged it from there? Wouldn't this free me from the telephone and get me to the typewriter?

Thus was the mythical city born.

Out of desperation, I guess.

I've never regretted the choice. If a conglomerate detective hero was something new in detective fiction, then the mythical city as a backdrop was similarly new. At least, I knew of no other writer who had used it before. Anyway, I thought it would be more fun to *create* a city than to write about an existing one. It has turned out to be a *lot* of fun. I can't describe how much joy I experience each time I write about another section of a city that doesn't exist, inventing historical background, naming places as suits my fancy, and then fitting it all together in a jigsaw pattern that sometimes even *I* don't fully understand. It is next to impossible to overlay a map of my city on a map of New York. It's not simply a matter of north being east and south being west or Isola representing Manhattan and Calm's Point representing Brooklyn. The geography won't jibe exactly, the city remains a mystery.

The city, then, became a character.

So did the weather, which figures prominently in *Cop Hater* and in each subsequent book in the series.

But there is one other character worth mentioning: the author.

I know that in these books I frequently commit the unpardonable sin of author intrusion. Somebody will suddenly start talking or thinking or commenting and it won't be any of the cops or crooks, it'll just be this faceless, anonymous "someone" sticking his nose into the proceedings like an unwanted guest. Sorry. That's me. Or rather, it's Ed McBain.

Where did the name come from?

Out of the blue.

I did not want to use Evan Hunter on the series; I

felt at the time that Evan Hunter was supposed to write so-called "serious" novels and maybe crime novels weren't serious enough. I now know they are very serious indeed, and many years ago I voluntarily blew the McBain cover (which really was a secret for a good long while). But neither did I want to use Marsten or Collins if this was to be a *new* series by a supposedly *new* writer.

I had just pulled the last page of *Cop Hater* out of the typewriter. I read the final lines, and sat there thinking for several moments. I used to work in the back bedroom of a development house on Long Island. I walked out of the bedroom, and into the kitchen, where my former wife was spoon-feeding our infant twins.

I said, "How's Ed McBain?"

She said, "Good," and went back to feeding the twins.

So here's *Cop Hater*. By Ed McBain.

The first of them.

Ed McBain

Cop Hater

1

From the river bounding the city on the north, you saw only the magnificent skyline. You stared up at it in something like awe, and sometimes you caught your breath because the view was one of majestic splendor. The clear silhouettes of the buildings slashed at the sky, devouring the blue; flat planes and long planes, rough rectangles and needle sharp spires, minarets and peaks, pattern upon pattern laid in geometric unity against the wash of blue and white which was the sky.

And at night, coming down the River Highway, you were caught in a dazzling galaxy of brilliant suns, a web of lights strung out from the river and then south to capture the city in a brilliant display of electrical wizardry. The highway lights glistened close and glistened farther as they skirted the city and reflected in the dark waters of the river. The windows of the buildings climbed in brilliant rectangular luminosity, climbed to the stars and joined the wash of red and green and yellow and orange neon which tinted the sky. The traffic lights blinked their gaudy eyes and along The Stem, the incandescent display tangled in a riot of color and eye-aching splash.

The city lay like a sparkling nest of rare gems, shimmering in layer upon layer of pulsating intensity.

The buildings were a stage set.

They faced the river, and they glowed with man-made brilliance, and you stared up at them in awe, and you caught your breath.

Behind the buildings, behind the lights, were the streets.

There was garbage in the streets.

The alarm sounded at eleven P.M.

He reached out for it, groping in the darkness, finding the lever and pressing it against the back of the clock. The buzzing stopped. The room was very silent. Beside him, he could hear May's even breathing. The windows were wide open, but the room was hot and damp, and he thought again about the air conditioning unit he'd wanted to buy since the summer began. Reluctantly, he sat up and rubbed ham-like fists into his eyes.

He was a big man, his head topped with straight blond hair that was unruly now. His eyes were normally grey, but they were virtually colorless in the darkness of the room, puffed with sleep. He stood up and stretched. He slept only in pajama pants, and when he raised his arms over his head, the pants slipped down over the flatness of his hard belly. He let out a grunt, pulled up the pants, and then glanced at May again.

The sheet was wadded at the foot of the bed, a soggy lifeless mass. May lay curled into a sprawling C, her gown twisted up over her thigh. He went to the bed and put his hand on her thigh for an instant. She murmured and rolled over. He grinned in the darkness and then went into the bathroom to shave.

He had timed every step of the operation, and so he knew just how long it took to shave, just how long it took to dress, just how long it took to gulp a quick cup of coffee. He took off his wristwatch before he began shaving, leaving it on the washbasin where he could glance at it occasionally. At eleven-ten, he began dressing. He put on an Aloha shirt his brother had sent him from Hawaii. He put on a pair of tan gabardine slacks, and a light poplin windbreaker. He put a handkerchief in his left hip pocket, and then scooped his wallet and change off the dresser.

He opened the top drawer of the dresser and took the .38 from where it lay next to May's jewelry box. His thumb passed over the hard leather of the holster, and then he shoved the holster and gun into his right hip pocket, beneath the poplin jacket. He lit a cigarette, went into the kitchen to put up the coffee water, and then went to check on the kids.

Mickey was asleep, his thumb in his mouth as usual. He passed his hand over the boy's head. Christ, he was sweating like a pig. He'd have to talk to May about the air conditioning again. It wasn't fair to the kids, cooped up like this in a sweat box. He walked to Cathy's bed and went through the

4
ED McBAIN

same ritual. She wasn't as perspired as her brother.
Well, she was a girl, girls didn't sweat as much. He
heard the kettle in the kitchen whistling loudly. He
glanced at his watch, and then grinned.

He went into the kitchen, spooned two teaspoon-
fuls of instant coffee into a large cup, and then
poured the boiling water over the powder. He drank
the coffee black, without sugar. He felt himself coming awake at last, and he vowed for the hundredth
time that he wouldn't try to catch any sleep before
this tour, it was plain stupid. He should sleep when
he got home, hell, what did he average this way? A
couple of hours? And then it was time to go in. No,
it was foolish. He'd have to talk to May about it. He
gulped the coffee down, and then went into his bedroom again.

He liked to look at her asleep. He always felt a little sneaky and a little horny when he took advantage
of her that way. Sleep was a kind of private thing,
and it wasn't right to pry when somebody was completely unaware. But, God, she was beautiful when
she was asleep, so what the hell, it wasn't fair. He
watched her for several moments, the dark hair
spread out over the pillow, the rich sweep of her hip
and thigh, the femaleness of the raised gown and
the exposed white flesh. He went to the side of the
bed, and brushed the hair back from her temple.
He kissed her very gently, but she stirred and said,
"Mike?"

"Go back to sleep, honey."

"Are you leaving?" she murmured hoarsely.

"Yes."

"Be careful, Mike."

"I will." He grinned. "And you be good."

"Uhm," she said, and then she rolled over into the pillow. He sneaked a last look at her from the doorway, and then went through the living room and out of the house. He glanced at his watch. It was eleventhirty. Right on schedule, and damn if it wasn't a lot cooler in the street.

At eleven forty-one, when Mike Reardon was three blocks away from his place of business, two bullets entered the back of his skull and ripped away half his face when they left his body. He felt only impact and sudden unbearable pain, and then vaguely heard the shots, and then everything inside him went dark, and he crumpled to the pavement.

He was dead before he struck the ground.

He had been a citizen of the city, and now his blood poured from his broken face and spread around him in a sticky red smear.

Another citizen found him at eleven fifty-six, and went to call the police. There was very little difference between the citizen who rushed down the street to a phone booth, and the citizen named Mike Reardon who lay crumpled and lifeless against the concrete.

Except one.

Mike Reardon was a cop.

2

The two Homicide cops looked down at the body on the sidewalk. It was a hot night, and the flies swarmed around the sticky blood on the pavement. The assistant medical examiner was kneeling alongside the body, gravely studying it. A photographer from the Bureau of Identification was busily popping flashbulbs. Cars 23 and 24 were parked across the street, and the patrolmen from those cars were unhappily engaged in keeping back spectators.

The call had gone to one of the two switchboards at Headquarters where a sleepy patrolman had listlessly taken down the information and then shot it via pneumatic tube to the Radio Room. The dispatcher in the Radio Room, after consulting the huge precinct map on the wall behind him, had sent Car 23 to investigate and report on the allegedly bleeding man in the street. When Car 23 had reported back with a homicide, the dispatcher had contacted Car 24 and sent it to the scene. At the same time, the patrolman on the switchboard had called Homicide North and also the 87th Precinct, in which territory the body had been found.

The body lay outside an abandoned, boarded-up theatre. The theatre had started as a first-run movie house, many years back when the neighborhood had still been fashionable. As the neighborhood began rotting, the theatre began showing second-run films, and then old movies, and finally foreign language films. There was a door to the left of the movie house, and the door had once been boarded, too, but the planks had been ripped loose and the staircase inside was littered with cigarette butts, empty pint whiskey bottles, and contraceptives. The marquee above the theatre stretched to the sidewalk, punched with jagged holes, the victim of thrown rocks, tin cans, hunks of pipe, and general debris.

Across the street from the theatre was an empty lot. The lot had once owned an apartment house, and the house had been a good one with high rents. It had not been unusual, in the old days, to see an occasional mink coat drifting from the marbled doorway of that apartment house. But the crawling tendrils of the slum had reached out for the brick, clutching it with tenacious fingers, pulling it into the ever-widening circle it called its own. The old building had succumbed, becoming a part of the slum, so that people rarely remembered it had once been a proud and elegant dwelling. And then it had been condemned, and the building had been razed to the ground, and now the lot was clear and open, except for the scattered brick rubble that still clung to the ground in some places. A city housing project, it was rumored, was going up in the lot. In the meantime, the kids used the lot for various purposes. Most of the purposes were concerned with bodily functions, and so a stench hung on the air over the lot, and the stench was particularly strong on a hot summer night, and it drifted over toward the theatre, captured beneath the canopy of the overhanging marquee, smothering the sidewalk with its smell of life, mingling with the smell of death on the pavement.

One of the Homicide cops moved away from the body and began scouring the sidewalk. The second cop stood with his hands in his back pockets. The assistant m.e. went through the ritual of ascertaining the death of a man who was certainly dead. The first cop came back.

"You see these?" he asked.

"What've you got?"

"Couple of ejected cartridge cases."

"Mm?"

"Remington slugs, .45 caliber."

"Put 'em in an envelope and tag 'em. You about finished, Doc?"

"In a minute."

The flashbulbs kept popping. The photographer worked like the press agent for a hit musical. He circled the star of the show, and he snapped his pictures from different angles, and all the while his face showed no expression, and the sweat streamed down his back, sticking his shirt to his flesh. The assistant m.e. ran his hand across his forehead.

"What the hell's keeping the boys from the 87th?" the first cop asked.

"Big poker game going, probably. We're better off without them." He turned to the assistant m.e. "What do you say, Doc?"

"I'm through." He rose wearily.

"What've you got?"

"Just what it looks like. He was shot twice in the back of the head. Death was probably instantaneous."

"Want to give us a time?"

"On a gunshot wound? Don't kid me."

"I thought you guys worked miracles."

"We do. But not during the summer."

"Can't you even guess?"

"Sure, guessing's free. No rigor mortis yet, so I'd say he was killed maybe a half-hour ago. With this heat, though ... hell, he might maintain normal body warmth for hours. You won't get us to go out on a limb with this one. Not even after the autopsy is ..."

"All right, all right. Mind if we find out who he is?"

"Just don't mess it up for the Lab boys. I'm taking off." The assistant m.e. glanced at his watch. "For the benefit of the timekeeper, it's 12:19."

"Short day today," the first Homicide cop said. He jotted the time down on the timetable he'd kept since his arrival at the scene.

The second cop was kneeling near the body. He looked up suddenly. "He's heeled," he said.

"Yeah?"

The assistant m.e. walked away, mopping his brow.

"Looks like a .38," the second cop said. He examined the holstered gun more closely. "Yeah. Detective's Special. Want to tag this?"

"Sure." The first cop heard a car brake to a stop across the street. The front doors opened, and two men stepped out and headed for the knot around the body. "Here's the 87th now."

"Just in time for tea," the second cop said dryly. "Who'd they send?"

"Looks like Carella and Bush." The first cop took a packet of rubber-banded tags from his right-hand jacket pocket. He slipped one of the tags free from the rubber band, and then returned the rest to his pocket. The tag was a three-by-five rectangle of an oatmeal color. A hole was punched in one end of the tag, and a thin wire was threaded through the hole and twisted to form two loose ends. The tag read POLICE DEPARTMENT, and beneath that in bolder type: EVIDENCE.

Carella and Bush, from the 87th Precinct, walked over leisurely. The Homicide cop glanced at them cursorily, turned to the *Where found* space on the tag, and began filling it out. Carella wore a blue suit, his grey tie neatly clasped to his white shirt. Bush was wearing an orange sports shirt and khaki trousers.

"If it ain't Speedy Gonzales and Whirlaway," the second Homicide cop said. "You guys certainly move fast, all right. What do you do on a bomb scare?"

"We leave it to the Bomb Squad," Carella said dryly. "What do you do?"

"You're very comical," the Homicide cop said.

"We got hung up."

"I can see that."

"I was catching alone when the squeal came in," Carella said. "Bush was out with Foster on a bar knifing. Reardon didn't show." Carella paused. "Ain't that right, Bush?" Bush nodded.

"If you're catching, what the hell are you doing here?" the first Homicide cop said.

Carella grinned. He was a big man, but not a heavy one. He gave an impression of great power, but the power was not a meaty one. It was, instead, a fine-honed muscular power. He wore his brown hair short. His eyes were brown, with a peculiar downward slant that gave him a clean-shaved Oriental appearance. He had wide shoulders and narrow hips, and he managed to look well-dressed and elegant even when he was dressed in a leather jacket for a waterfront plant. He had thick wrists and big hands, and he spread the hands wide now and said, "Me answer the phone when there's a homicide in progress?" His grin widened. "I left Foster to catch. Hell, he's practically a rookie."

"How's the graft these days?" the second Homicide cop asked.

"Up yours," Carella answered dryly.

"Some guys get all the luck. You sure as hell don't get anything from a stiff."

"Except *tsores,*" the first cop said.

"Talk English," Bush said genially. He was a soft-spoken man, and his quiet voice came as a surprise because he was all of six-feet-four-inches and

weighed at least two-twenty, bone dry. His hair
was wild and unkempt, as if a wise Providence
had fashioned his unruly thatch after his surname.
His hair was also red, and it clashed violently
against the orange sports shirt he wore. His arms
hung from the sleeves of the shirt, muscular and
thick. A jagged knife scar ran the length of his
right arm.

The photographer walked over to where the detectives were chatting.

"What the hell are you doing?" he asked angrily.

"We're trying to find out who he is," the second
cop said. "Why? What's the matter?"

"I didn't say I was finished with him yet."

"Well, ain't you?"

"Yeah, but you should've asked."

"For Christ's sake, who are you working for?
Conover?"

"You Homicide dicks give me a pain in the . . ."

"Go home and emulsify some negatives or something, will you?"

The photographer glanced at his watch. He
grunted and withheld the time purposely, so that
the first cop had to glance at his own watch before
jotting down the time on his timetable. He sub-
tracted a few minutes, and indicated a t.o.a. for
Carella and Bush, too.

Carella looked down at the back of the dead
man's head. His face remained expressionless, except for a faint, passing film of pain which covered
his eyes for a moment, and then darted away as
fleetingly as a jackrabbit.

"What'd they use?" he asked. "A cannon?"

"A .45," the first cop said. "We've got the cartridge cases."

"How many?"

"Two."

"Figures," Carella said. "Why don't we flip him over?"

"Ambulance coming?" Bush asked quietly.

"Yeah," the first cop said. "Everybody's late tonight."

"Everybody's drowning in sweat tonight," Bush said. "I can use a beer."

"Come on," Carella said, "give me a hand here."

The second cop bent down to help Carella. Together, they rolled the body over. The flies swarmed up angrily, and then descended to the sidewalk again, and to the bloody broken flesh that had once been a face. In the darkness, Carella saw a gaping hole where the left eye should have been. There was another hole beneath the right eye, and the cheekbone was splintered outward, the jagged shards piercing the skin.

"Poor bastard," Carella said. He would never get used to staring death in the face. He had been a cop for twelve years now, and he had learned to stomach the sheer, overwhelming, physical impact of death— but he would never get used to the other thing about death, the invasion of privacy that came with death, the reduction of pulsating life to a pile of bloody, fleshy rubbish.

"Anybody got a flash?" Bush asked.

The first cop reached into his left hip pocket. He

thumbed a button, and a circle of light splashed onto the sidewalk.

"On his face," Bush said.

The light swung up onto the dead man's face.

Bush swallowed. "That's Reardon," he said, his voice very quiet. And then, almost in a whisper, "Jesus, that's Mike Reardon."

3

There were sixteen detectives assigned to the 87th Precinct, and David Foster was one of them. The precinct, in all truth, could have used a hundred and sixteen detectives and even then been understaffed. The precinct area spread south from the River Highway and the tall buildings which still boasted doormen and elevator operators to the Stem with its delicatessens and movie houses, on south to Culver Avenue and the Irish section, still south to the Puerto Rican section and then into Grover's Park, where muggers and rapists ran rife. Running east and west, the precinct covered a long total of some thirty-five city streets. And packed into this rectangle—north and south from the river to the park, east and west for thirty-five blocks—was a population of 90,000 people.

David Foster was one of those people.

David Foster was a Negro.

He had been born in the precinct territory, and he had grown up there, and when he'd turned 21, being of sound mind and body, being four inches over the minimum requirement of five feet eight inches, having 20/20 vision without glasses, and not having any criminal record, he had taken the competitive Civil Service examination and had been appointed a patrolman.

The starting salary at the time had been $3,725 per annum, and Foster had earned his salary well. He had earned it so well that in the space of five years he had been appointed to the Detective Division. He was now a 3rd Grade Detective, and his salary was now $5,230 per annum, and he still earned it.

At one A.M., on the morning of July 24th, while a colleague named Mike Reardon lay spilling his blood into the gutter, David Foster was earning his salary by interrogating the man he and Bush had picked up in the bar knifing.

The interrogation was being conducted on the second floor of the precinct house. To the right of the desk on the first floor, there was an inconspicuous and dirty white sign with black letters which announced DETECTIVE DIVISION, and a pointing hand advised any visitor that the bulls hung out upstairs.

The stairs were metal, and narrow, but scrupulously clean. They went up for a total of sixteen risers, then turned back on themselves and continued on up for another sixteen risers, and there you were.

Where you were was a narrow, dimly lit corridor. There were two doors on the right of the open stairway, and a sign labeled them LOCKERS. If you turned left and walked down the corridor, you

passed a wooden slatted bench on your left, a bench
without a back on your right (set into a narrow al-
cove before the sealed doors of what had once been
an elevator shaft), a door on your right marked
MEN'S LAVATORY, and a door on your left over which a
small sign hung, and the sign simply read CLERICAL.

At the end of the corridor was the Detective
Squad Room.

You saw first a slatted rail divider. Beyond that,
you saw desks and telephones, and a bulletin board
with various photographs and notices on it, and a
hanging light globe and beyond that more desks
and the grilled windows that opened on the front of
the building. You couldn't see very much that went
on beyond the railing on your right because two
huge metal filing cabinets blocked the desks on that
side of the room. It was on that side of the room
that Foster was interrogating the man he'd picked
up in the bar earlier that night.

"What's your name?" he asked the man.

"No hablo inglés," the man said.

"Oh, hell," Foster said. He was a burly man with a
deep chocolate coloring and warm brown eyes. He
wore a white dress shirt, open at the throat. His
sleeves were rolled up over muscular forearms.

"Cuál es su nombre?" he asked in hesitant Spanish.

"Tomas Perillo."

"Your address?" He paused, thinking. *"Dirección?"*

"Tres-tres-cuatro Mei-son."

"Age? *Edad?"*

Perillo shrugged.

"All right," Foster said, "where's the knife? Oh,

crap, we'll never get anywhere tonight. Look, *dónde
está el cuchillo? Puede usted decirme?*"

"*Creo que no.*"

"Why not? For Christ's sake, you had a knife,
didn't you?"

"*No sé.*"

"Look, you son of a bitch, you know damn well
you had a knife. A dozen people saw you with it.
Now how about it?"

Perillo was silent.

"*Tiene usted un cuchillo?*" Foster asked.

"*No.*"

"You're a liar!" Foster said. "You *do* have a knife.
What'd you do with it after you slashed that guy in
the bar?"

"*Dónde está el servicio?*" Perillo asked.

"Never mind where the hell the men's room is,"
Foster snapped. "Stand up straight, for Christ's sake.
What the hell do you think this is, the pool room?
Take your hands out of your pockets."

Perillo took his hands from his pockets.

"Now where's the knife?"

"*No sé.*"

"You don't know, you don't know," Foster mim-
icked. "All right, get the hell out of here. Sit down
on the bench outside. I'm gonna get a cop in here
who really speaks your language, pal. Now go sit
down. Go ahead."

"*Bien,*" Perillo said. "*Dónde está el servicio?*"

"Down the hall on your left. And don't take all
night in there."

Perillo went out. Foster grimaced. The man he'd

cut hadn't been cut bad at all. If they knocked themselves out over every goddamn knifing they got, they'd be busy running down nothing but knifings. He wondered what it would be like to be stationed in a precinct where carving was something you did to a turkey. He grinned at his own humor, wheeled a typewriter over, and began typing up a report on the burglary they'd had several days back.

When Carella and Bush came in, they seemed in a big hurry. Carella walked directly to the phone, consulted a list of phone numbers beside it, and began dialing.

"What's up?" Foster said.

"That homicide," Carella answered.

"Yeah?"

"It was Mike."

"What do you mean? Huh?"

"Mike Reardon."

"What?" Foster said. "What?"

"Two slugs at the back of his head. I'm calling the lieutenant. He's gonna want to move fast on this one."

"Hey, is he kidding?" Foster said to Bush, and then he saw the look on Bush's face, and he knew this was not a joke.

Lieutenant Byrnes was the man in charge of the 87th Detective Squad. He had a small, compact body and a head like a rivet. His eyes were blue and tiny, but those eyes had seen a hell of a lot, and they didn't miss very much that went on around the lieutenant. The lieutenant knew his precinct was a trou-

ble spot, and that was the way he liked it. It was the
bad neighborhoods that needed policemen, he was
fond of saying, and he was proud to be a part of a
squad that really earned its keep. There had once
been sixteen men in his squad, and now there were
fifteen.

Ten of those fifteen were gathered around him in
the squad room, the remaining five being out on
plants from which they could not be yanked. The
men sat in their chairs, or on the edges of desks, or
they stood near the grilled windows, or they leaned
against filing cabinets. The squad room looked the
way it might look at any of the times when the new
shift was coming in to relieve the old one, except
that there were no dirty jokes now. The men all
knew that Mike Reardon was dead.

Acting Lieutenant Lynch stood alongside Byrnes
while Byrnes filled his pipe. Byrnes had thick capable fingers, and he wadded the tobacco with his
thumb, not looking up at the men.

Carella watched him. Carella admired and re-
spected the lieutenant, even though many of the
other men called him "an old turd." Carella knew
cops who worked in precincts where the old man
wielded a whip instead of a cerebellum. It wasn't
good to work for a tyrant. Byrnes was all right, and
Byrnes was also a good cop and a smart cop, and so
Carella gave him his undivided attention, even
though the lieutenant had not yet begun speaking.

Byrnes struck a wooden match and lighted his
pipe. He gave the appearance of an unhurried man
about to take his port after a heavy meal, but the

wheels were grinding furiously inside his compact skull, and every fiber in his body was outraged at the death of one of his best men.

"No pep talk," he said suddenly. "Just go out and find the bastard." He blew out a cloud of smoke and then waved it away with one of his short, wide hands. "If you read the newspapers, and if you start believing them, you'll know that cops hate cop killers. That's the law of the jungle. That's the law of survival. The newspapers are full of crap if they think any revenge motive is attached. We can't let a cop be killed because a cop is a symbol of law and order. If you take away the symbol, you get animals in the streets. We've got enough animals in the streets now.

"So I want you to find Reardon's killer, but not because Reardon was a cop assigned to this precinct, and not even because Reardon was a good cop. I want you to find that bastard because Reardon was a *man*—and a damned fine man.

"Handle it however you want to, you know your jobs. Give me progress reports on whatever you get from the files, and whatever you get in the streets. But find him. That's all."

The lieutenant went back into his office with Lynch, and some of the cops went to the Modus Operandi file and began digging for information on thugs who used .45's. Some of the cops went to the Lousy file, the file of known criminals in the precinct, and they began searching for any cheap thieves who may have crossed Mike Reardon's path at one time or another. Some of the cops went to the Convictions file and began a methodical search of cards listing every conviction for which the precinct had been responsible, with a special eye out for cases on which Mike Reardon had worked. Foster went out into the corridor and told the suspect he'd questioned to get the hell home and to keep his nose clean. The rest of the cops took to the streets, and Carella and Bush were among them.

"He gripes my ass," Bush said. "He thinks he's Napoleon."

"He's a good man," Carella said.

"Well, *he* seems to think so, anyway."

"Everything gripes you," Carella said. "You're maladjusted."

"I'll tell you one thing," Bush said. "I'm getting an ulcer in this goddamn precinct. I never had trouble before, but since I got assigned to this precinct, I'm getting an ulcer. Now how do you account for that?"

There were a good many possible ways to account for Bush's ulcer and none of them had anything whatever to do with the precinct. But Carella didn't feel like arguing at the moment, and so he kept his peace. Bush simply nodded sourly.

"I want to call my wife," he said.

"At two in the morning?" Carella asked incredulously.

"What's the matter with that?" Bush wanted to know. He was suddenly antagonistic.

"Nothing. Go ahead, call her."

"I just want to check," Bush said, and then he said, "Check in."

"Sure."

"Hell, we may be going for days on this one."

"Sure."

"Anything wrong with calling her to let her know what's up?"

"Listen, are you looking for an argument?" Carella asked, smiling.

"No."

"Then go call your wife, and get the hell off my back."

Bush nodded emphatically. They stopped outside an open candy store on Culver, and Bush went in to make his call. Carella stood outside, his back to the open counter at the store's front.

The city was very quiet. The tenements stretched grimy fingers toward the soft muzzle of the sky. Occasionally, a bathroom light winked like an opening eye in an otherwise blinded face. Two young Irish girls walked past the candy store, their high heels clattering on the pavement. He glanced momentarily at their legs and the thin summer frocks they wore. One of the girls winked unashamedly at him, and then both girls began giggling, and for no good reason he remembered something about lifting the skirts of an Irish lass, and the thought came to him full-blown so that he knew it was stored somewhere in his memory, and it seemed to him he had read it. Irish lasses, *Ulysses*? Christ, that had been one hell of a book to get through, pretty little lasses and all. I wonder what Bush reads? Bush is too busy to read. Bush is too busy worrying about his wife. Jesus, does that man worry.

He glanced over his shoulder. Bush was still in the

booth, talking rapidly. The man behind the counter
leaned over a racing form, a toothpick angling up
out of his mouth. A young kid sat at the end of the
counter drinking an egg cream. Carella sucked in a
breath of fetid air. The door to the phone booth
opened, and Bush stepped out, mopping his brow.
He nodded at the counterman, and then went out
to join Carella.

"Hot as hell in that booth," he said.

"Everything okay?" Carella asked.

"Sure," Bush said. He looked at Carella suspiciously. "Why shouldn't it be?"

"No reason. Any ideas where we should start?"

"This isn't going to be such a cinch," Bush said.
"Any stupid son of a bitch with a grudge could've
done it."

"Or anybody in the middle of committing a
crime."

"We ought to leave it to Homicide. We're in over
our heads."

"We haven't even started yet, and you say we're in
over our heads. What the hell's wrong with you,
Hank?"

"Nothing," Bush said, "only I don't happen to
think of cops as masterminds, that's all."

"That's a nice thing for a cop to say."

"It's the truth. Look, this detective tag is a bunch
of crap, and you know it as well as I do. All you
need to be a detective is a strong pair of legs, and a
stubborn streak. The legs take you around to all the
various dumps you have to go to, and the stubborn
streak keeps you from quitting. You follow each sep-

arate trail mechanically, and if you're lucky, one of the trails pays off. If you're not lucky, it doesn't. Period."

"And brains don't enter into it at all, huh?"

"Only a little. It doesn't take much brains to be a cop."

"Okay."

"Okay what?"

"Okay, I don't want to argue. If Reardon got it trying to stop somebody in the commission of a crime . . ."

"That's another thing that burns me up about cops," Bush said.

"You're a regular cop hater, aren't you?" Carella asked.

"This whole goddamn city is full of cop haters. You think anybody respects a cop? Symbol of law and order, crap! The old man ought to get out there and face life. Anybody who ever got a parking tag is automatically a cop hater. That's the way it is."

"Well, it sure as hell shouldn't be that way," Carella said, somewhat angrily.

Bush shrugged. "What burns me up about cops is they don't speak English."

"What?"

"In the commission of a crime!" Bush mocked. "Cop talk. Did you ever hear a cop say 'We caught him?' No. He says, 'We apprehended him.' "

"I never heard a cop say 'We apprehended him,' " Carella said.

"I'm talking about for official publication," Bush said.

"Well, that's different. Everybody talks fancy when it's for official publication."

"Cops especially."

"Why don't you turn in your shield? Become a hackie or something?"

"I'm toying with the idea." Bush smiled suddenly. His entire tirade had been delivered in his normally hushed voice, and now that he was smiling, it was difficult to remember that he'd been angry at all.

"Anyway, I thought the bars," Carella said. "I mean, if this *is* a grudge kind of thing, it might've been somebody from the neighborhood. And we may be able to pick up something in the bars. Who the hell knows?"

"I can use a beer, anyway," Bush said. "I've been wanting a beer ever since I come on tonight."

The Shamrock was one of a million bars all over the world with the same name. It squatted on Culver Avenue between a pawn shop and a Chinese laundry. It was an all-night joint, and it catered to the Irish clientele that lined Culver. Occasionally, a Puerto Rican wandered into *The Shamrock,* but such offtrail excursions were discouraged by those among *The Shamrock's* customers who owned quick tempers and powerful fists. The cops stopped at the bar often, not to wet their whistles—because drinking on duty was strictly forbidden by the rules and regulations— but to make sure that too many quick tempers did not mix with too much whiskey or too many fists. The flare-ups within the gaily decorated walls of the bar were now few and far between, or—to be poetic—less frequent than they had been in the good old days when the neighborhood had first succumbed to the Puerto Rican assault wave. In those days, not speaking English too well, not reading signs too well, the Puerto Ricans stumbled into *The Shamrock* with remarkably ignorant rapidity. The staunch defenders of America for the Americans, casually ignoring the fact that Puerto Ricans were and are Americans, spent many a pugilistic evening proving their point. The bar was often brilliantly decorated with spilled blood. But that was in the good old days. In the bad new days, you could go into *The Shamrock* for a week running, and not see more than one or two broken heads.

There was a Ladies Invited sign in the window of the bar, but not many ladies accepted the invitation. The drinkers were, instead, neighborhood men who tired of the four walls of their dreary tenement flats, who sought the carefree camaraderie of other men who had similarly grown weary of their own homes. Their wives were out playing Bingo on Tuesdays, or at the movies collecting a piece of china on Wednesdays, or across the street with the Sewing Club ("We so and so and so and so") on Thursdays, and so it went. So what was wrong with a friendly brew in a neighborhood tavern? Nothing.

Except when the cops showed.

Now there was something very disgusting about policemen in general, and bulls in particular. Sure, you could go through the motions of saying, "How are yuh this evenin', Officer Dugan?" and all that sort of rot, and you could really and truly maybe hold a fond spot in the old ticker for the new rookie, but you still couldn't deny that a cop sitting next to you when you were halfway toward getting a snootful was a somewhat disconcerting thing and would likely bring on the goblins in the morning. Not that anyone had anything against cops. It was just that cops should not loiter around bars and spoil a man's earnest drinking. Nor should cops hang around book joints and spoil a man's earnest gambling. Nor should they hang around brothels and spoil a man's earnest endeavors to, cops simply shouldn't hang around, that was all.

And bulls, bulls were cops in disguise, only worse.

So what did those two big jerks at the end of the bar want?

"A beer, Harry," Bush said.

"Comin' up," Harry the bartender answered. He drew the beer and brought it over to where Bush and Carella were seated. "Good night for a beer, ain't it?" Harry said.

"I never knew a bartender who didn't give you a commercial when you ordered a beer on a hot night," Bush said quietly.

Harry laughed, but only because his customer was a cop. Two men at the shuffleboard table were arguing about an Irish free state. The late movie on television was about a Russian empress.

"You fellows here on business?" Harry asked.

"Why?" Bush said. "You got any for us?"

"No, I was just wonderin'. I mean, it ain't often we get the bu . . . it ain't often a detective drops by," Harry said.

"That's because you run such a clean establishment," Bush said.

"Ain't none cleaner on Culver."

"Not since they ripped your phone booth out," Bush said.

"Yeah, well, we were gettin' too many phone calls."

"You were taking too many bets," Bush said, his voice even. He picked up the glass of beer, dipped his upper lip into the foam, and then downed it.

"No, no kiddin'," Harry said. He did not like to think of the close call he'd had with that damn phone booth and the State Attorney's Commission. "You fellows lookin' for somebody?"

"Kind of quiet tonight," Carella said.

Harry smiled, and a gold tooth flashed at the front of his mouth. "Oh, always quiet in here, fellows, you know that."

"Sure," Carella said, nodding. "Danny Gimp drop in?"

"No, haven't seen him tonight. Why? What's up?"

"That's good beer," Bush said.

"Like another?"

"No, thanks."

"Say, are you sure nothing's wrong?" Harry asked.

"What's with you, Harry? Somebody do something wrong here?" Carella asked.

"What? No, hey no, I hope I didn't give you that impression. It's just kind of strange, you fellows dropping in. I mean, we haven't had any trouble here or anything."

"Well, that's good," Carella said. "See anybody with a gun lately?"

"A gun?"

"Yeah."

"What kind of a gun?"

"What kind did you see?"

"I didn't see any kind." Harry was sweating. He drew a beer for himself and drank it hastily.

"None of the young punks in with zip guns or anything?" Bush asked quietly.

"Oh, well zip guns," Harry said, wiping the foam from his lip, "I mean, you see them all the time."

"And nothing bigger?"

"Bigger like what? Like you mean a .32 or a .38?"

"Like we mean a .45," Carella said.

"The last .45 I seen in here," Harry said, thinking, "was away back in . . ." He shook his head. "No, that wouldn't help you. What happened? Somebody get shot?"

"Away back *when?*" Bush asked.

"Fifty, fifty-one, it must've been. Kid discharged from the Army. Come in here wavin' a .45 around. He was lookin' for trouble, all right, that kid. Dooley busted it up. You remember Dooley? He used to have this beat before he got transferred out to another precinct. Nice kid. Always used to stop by and . . ."

"He still live in the neighborhood?" Bush asked.

"Huh? Who?"

"The guy who was in here waving the .45 around."

"Oh, him." Harry's brows swooped down over his eyes. "Why?"

"I'm asking you," Bush said. "Does he or doesn't he?"

"Yeah. I guess. Why?"

"Where?"

"Listen," Harry said, "I don't want to get nobody in trouble."

"You're not getting anybody in trouble," Bush said. "Does this guy still own the .45?"

"I don't know."

"What happened that night? When Dooley busted it up."

"Nothing. The kid had a load on. You know, just out of the Army, like that."

"Like what?"

"Like he was wavin' the gun around. I don't even think it was loaded. I think the barrel was leaded."

"Are you sure it was?"

"Well, no."

"Did Dooley take the gun away from him?"

"Well . . ." Harry paused and mopped his brow. "Well, I don't think Dooley even saw the gun."

"If he busted it up . . ."

"Well," Harry said, "one of the fellows saw Dooley comin' down the street, and they kind of calmed the kid down and got him out of here."

"*Before* Dooley came in?"

"Well, yeah. Yeah."

"And the kid took the gun with him when he left?"

"Yeah," Harry said. "Look, I didn't want no trouble in my place, you follow?"

"I follow," Bush said. "Where does he live?"

Harry blinked his eyes. He looked down at the bar top.

"Where?" Bush repeated.

"On Culver."

"Where on Culver?"

"The house on the corner of Culver and Mason. Look, fellows . . ."

"This guy mention anything about not liking cops?" Carella asked.

"No, no," Harry said. "He's a fine boy. He just had a couple of sheets to the wind that night, that's all."

"You know Mike Reardon?"

"Oh, sure," Harry said.

"This kid know Mike?"

"Well, I can't say as I know. Look, the kid was just squiffed that night, that's all."

"What's his name?"

"Look, he was only tanked up, that's all. Hell, it was away back in 1950."

"What's his name?"

"Frank. Frank Clarke. With an 'e'."

"What do you think, Steve?" Bush asked Carella.

Carella shrugged. "It came too easy. It's never good when it comes that easy."

"Let's check it anyway," Bush said.

4

There are smells inside a tenement, and they are not only the smell of cabbage. The smell of cabbage, to many, is and always will be a good wholesome smell and there are many who resent the steady propaganda which links cabbage with poverty.

The smell inside a tenement is the smell of life.

It is the smell of every function of life, the sweating, the cooking, the elimination, the breeding. It is all these smells, and they are wedded into one gigantic smell which hits the nostrils the moment you enter the downstairs doorway. For the smell has been inside the building for decades. It has seeped through the floorboards and permeated the walls. It clings to the banister and the linoleum covered steps. It crouches in corners and it hovers about the naked light bulbs on each landing. The smell is always there, day and night. It is the stench of living, and it never sees the light of day, and it never sees the crisp brittleness of starlight.

It was there on the morning of July 24th at 3:00

A.M. It was there in full force because the heat of the day had baked it into the walls. It hit Carella as he and Bush entered the building. He snorted through his nostrils and then struck a match and held it to the mailboxes.

"There it is," Bush said. "Clarke. 3B."

Carella shook out the match and they walked toward the steps. The garbage cans were in for the night, stacked on the ground floor landing behind the steps. Their aroma joined the other smells to clash in a medley of putridity. The building slept, but the smells were awake. On the second floor, a man—or a woman—snored loudly. On each door, close to the floor, the circular trap for a milk bottle lock hung despondently, awaiting the milkman's arrival. On one of the doors hung a plaque, and the plaque read IN GOD WE TRUST. And behind that door, there was undoubtedly the unbending steel bar of a police lock, embedded in the floor and tilted to lean against the door.

Carella and Bush labored up to the third floor. The light bulb on the third floor landing was out. Bush struck a match.

"Down the hall there."

"You want to do this up big?" Carella asked.

"He's got a .45 in there, hasn't he?"

"Still."

"What the hell, my wife doesn't need my insurance money," Bush said.

They walked to the door and flanked it. They drew their service revolvers with nonchalance. Carella didn't for a moment believe he'd need his gun, but caution never hurt. He drew back his left hand and knocked on the door.

"Probably asleep," Bush said.

"Betokens a clear conscience," Carella answered. He knocked again.

"Who is it?" a voice answered.

"Police. Want to open up?"

"Oh, for Christ's sake," the voice mumbled. "Just a minute."

"We won't need these," Bush said. He holstered his gun, and Carella followed suit. From within the apartment, they could hear bed springs creaking, and then a woman's voice asking, "What is it?" They heard footsteps approaching the door, and then someone fumbled with the police lock on the inside, and the heavy steel bar clattered when it was dropped to the floor. The door opened a crack.

"What do you want?" the voice said.

"Police. We'd like to ask you a few questions."

"At this time of the morning? Jesus Christ, can't it wait?"

"Afraid it can't."

"Well, what's the matter? There a burglar in the building?"

"No. We'd just like to ask you some questions. You're Frank Clarke, aren't you?"

"Yeah." Clarke paused. "Let me see your badge."

Carella reached into his pocket for the leather case to which his shield was pinned. He held it up to the crack in the door.

"I can't see nothing," Clarke said. "Just a minute."

"Who is it?" the woman asked.

"The cops," Clarke mumbled. He stepped away from the door, and then a light flashed inside the apartment. He came back to the door. Carella held up the badge again.

"Yeah, okay," Clarke said. "What do you want?"

"You own a .45, Clarke?"

"What?"

"A .45. Do you own one?"

"Jesus, is that what you want to know? Is that what you come banging on the door for in the middle of the night? Ain't you guys got any sense at all? I got to go to work in the morning."

"Do you have a .45, or don't you?"

"Who said I had one?"

"Never mind who. How about it?"

"Why do you want to know? I been here all night."

"Anybody to swear for that?"

Clarke's voice lowered. "Hey, look, fellows, I got somebody with me, you know what I mean? Look, give me a break, will you?"

"What about the gun?"

"Yeah, I got one."

"A .45?"

"Yeah. Yeah, it's a .45."

"Mind if we take a look at it?"

"What for? I've got a permit for it."

"We'd like to look at it anyway."

"Hey, look, what the hell kind of a routine is this, anyway? I told you I got a permit for the gun. What did I do wrong? Whatya want from me, anyway?"

"We want to see the .45," Bush said. "Get it."

"You got a search warrant?" Clarke asked.

"Never mind the crap," Bush said. "Get the gun."

"You can't come in here without a search warrant. And you can't bulldoze me into gettin' the gun, either. I don't want to get that gun, then you can whistle."

"How old's the girl in there?" Bush asked.

"What?"

"You heard me. Wake up, Clarke!"

"She's 21, and you're barkin' up the wrong tree," Clarke said. "We're engaged."

From down the hall, someone shouted, "Hey, shut up, will ya? For Christ's sake! Go down to the poolroom, you want to talk!"

"How about letting us in, Clarke?" Carella asked gently. "We're waking your neighbors."

"I don't have to let you in noplace. Go get a search warrant."

"I know you don't, Clarke. But a cop's been killed, and he was killed with a .45, and if I were you I wouldn't play this so goddamn cozy. Now how about opening that door and showing us you're clean? How about it, Clarke?"

"A cop? Jesus, a cop! Jesus, why didn't you say so? Just a . . . just a minute, willya? Just a minute." He moved away from the door. Carella could hear him talking to the woman, and he could hear the woman's whispered answer. Clarke came back to the door and took off the night chain. "Come on in," he said.

There were dishes stacked in the kitchen sink. The kitchen was a six-by-eight rectangle, and adjoining that was the bedroom. The girl stood in the bed-

room doorway. She was a short blonde, somewhat
dumpy. She wore a man's bathrobe. Her eyes were
puffed with sleep, and she wore no makeup. She
blinked her eyes and stared at Carella and Bush as
they moved into the kitchen.

Clarke was a short man with bushy black brows
and brown eyes. His nose was long, broken sharply
in the middle. His lips were thick, and he needed a
shave badly. He was wearing pajama pants and nothing else. He stood bare-chested and bare-footed in
the glare of the kitchen light. The water tap dripped
its tattoo onto the dirty dishes in the sink.

"Let's see the gun," Bush said.

"I got a permit for it," Clarke answered. "Okay if I
smoke?"

"It's your apartment."

"Gladys," Clarke said, "there's a pack on the dresser. Bring some matches, too, willya?" The girl moved
into the darkness of the bedroom, and Clarke whispered, "You guys sure picked a hell of a time to
come calling, all right." He tried to smile, but neither Carella nor Bush seemed amused, and so he
dropped it instantly. The girl came back with the
package of cigarettes. She hung one on her lip, and
then handed the pack to Clarke. He lighted his own
cigarette and then handed the matches to the
blonde.

"What kind of a permit?" Carella asked. "Carry or
premises?"

"Carry," Clarke said.

"How come?"

"Well, it used to be premises. I registered the gun

when I got out of the Army. It was a gift," he said quickly. "From my captain."

"Go ahead."

"So I got a premises permit when I was discharged. That's the law, ain't it?"

"You're telling the story," Bush said.

"Well, that's the way I understood it. Either that, or I had to get the barrel leaded up. I don't remember. Anyway, I got the permit."

"*Is* the barrel leaded?"

"Hell, no. What do I need a permit for a dead gun for? I had this premises permit, and then I got a job with a jeweler, you know? Like I had to make a lot of valuable deliveries, things like that. So I had it changed to a carry permit."

"When was this?"

"Couple of months back."

"Which jeweler do you work for?"

"I quit that job," Clarke said.

"All right, get the gun. And get the permit, too, while you're at it."

"Sure," Clarke said. He went to the sink, held his cigarette under the dripping tap, and then dropped the soggy butt in with the dishes. He walked past the girl and into the bedroom.

"This is some time of night to be asking questions," the girl said angrily.

"We're sorry, Miss," Carella said.

"Yeah, I'll bet you are."

"We didn't mean to disturb your beauty sleep," Bush said nastily.

The girl raised one eyebrow. "Then why did you?"

She blew out a cloud of smoke, the way she had seen movie sirens do. Clarke came back into the room holding the .45. Bush's hand moved imperceptibly toward his right hip and the holster there.

"Put it on the table," Carella said.

Clarke put the gun on the table.

"Is it loaded?" Carella asked.

"I think so."

"Don't you know?"

"I ain't even looked at the thing since I quit that job."

Carella draped a handkerchief over his spread fingers and picked up the gun. He slid the magazine out. "It's loaded, all right," he said. Quickly, he sniffed the barrel.

"You don't have to smell," Clarke said. "It ain't been fired since I got out of the Army."

"It came close once, though, didn't it?"

"Huh?"

"That night in *The Shamrock.*"

"Oh, that," Clarke said. "Is that why you're here? Hell, I was looped that night. I didn't mean no harm."

Carella slammed the magazine back into place. "Where's the permit, Clarke?"

"Oh, yeah. I looked around in there. I couldn't find it."

"You're sure you've got one?"

"Yeah, I'm sure. I just can't find it."

"You'd better take another look. A good one, this time."

"I did take a good look. I can't find it. Look, I got

a permit. You can check on it. I wouldn't kid you. Who was the cop got killed?"

"Want to take another look for that permit?"

"I already told you, I can't find it. Look, I got one."

"You *had* one, pal," Carella said. "You just lost it."

"Huh? What? What'd you say?"

"When a cop asks you for your permit, you produce it or you lose it."

"Well, Jesus, I just misplaced it temporarily. Look, you can check all this. I mean . . . look, what's the matter with you guys, anyway? I didn't do nothing. I been here all night. You can ask Gladys. Ain't that right, Gladys?"

"He's been here all night," Gladys said.

"We're taking the gun," Carella said. "Give him a receipt for it, Hank."

"That ain't been fired in years," Clarke said. "You'll see. And you check on that permit. I got one. You check on it."

"We'll let you know," Carella said. "You weren't planning on leaving the city, were you?"

"What?"

"You weren't plan . . ."

"Hell, no. Where would I go?"

"Back to sleep is as good a place as any," the blonde said.

5

The pistol permit was on Steve Carella's desk when he reported for work at 4:00 P.M. on the afternoon of July 24th. He had worked until eight in the morning, gone home for six hours sleep, and was back at his desk now, looking a little bleary-eyed but otherwise none the worse for wear.

The heat had persisted all day long, a heavy yellow blanket that smothered the city in its woolly grip. Carella did not like the heat. He had never liked summer, even as a kid, and now that he was an adult and a cop, the only memorable characteristic summer seemed to have was that it made dead bodies stink quicker.

He loosened his collar the instant he entered the squad room, and when he got to his desk, he rolled up his sleeves, and then picked up the pistol permit.

Quickly, he scanned the printed form:

License No.	Date	Police Department	Year	(CARRY) PREMISES

PISTOL LICENSE APPLICATION

(APPLICATION MUST BE MADE IN DUPLICATE)

I Hereby Apply for License to
      Carry a Revolver or Pistol upon my person or
      Possession on premises _____
      37-12 Culver Avenue

For the following reasons: Make deliveries for
jewelry firm.

Clarke	Francis	D.	37-12 Culver Ave.
(PRINT) Surname	Given Name	Initials	Number Street

There was more, a lot more, but it didn't interest
Carella. Clarke had indeed owned a pistol permit—
but that didn't mean he hadn't used the pistol on a
cop named Mike Reardon.

Carella shoved the permit to one side of his desk,
glanced at his watch, and then reached for the
phone automatically. Quickly, he dialed Bush's
home number and then waited, his hand sweating
on the receiver. The phone rang six times, and then
a woman's voice said, "Hello?"

"Alice?"

"Who's this?"

"Steve Carella."

"Oh. Hello, Steve."

"Did I wake you?"

"Yes."

"Hank's not here yet. He's all right, isn't he?"

"He left a little while ago," Alice said. The sleep was
beginning to leave her voice already. Alice Bush was a

cop's wife who generally slept when her husband did,
adjusting her schedule to fit his. Carella had spoken
to her on a good many mornings and afternoons,
and he always marveled at the way she could come almost instantly awake within the space of three or four
sentences. Her voice invariably sounded like the first
faint rattle of impending death when she picked up
the receiver. As the conversation progressed, it mod-
ulated into the dulcet whine of a middle-aged Aire-
dale, and then into the disconcertingly sexy voice
which was the normal speaking voice of Hank's wife.
Carella had met her on one occasion, when he and
Hank had shared a late snack with her, and he knew
that she was a dynamic blonde with a magnificent figure and the brownest eyes he'd ever seen. From what
Bush had expansively delivered about personal aspects of his home life, Carella knew that Alice slept in
clinging black, sheer nightgowns. The knowledge was
unnerving, for whenever Carella roused her out of
bed, he automatically formed a mental picture of the
well-rounded blonde he'd met, and the picture was
always dressed as Hank had described it.

He generally, therefore, cut his conversations with
Alice short, feeling somewhat guilty about the artis-
tic inclinations of his mind. This morning, though,
Alice seemed to be in a talkative mood.

"I understand one of your colleagues got knocked
off," she said.

Carella smiled, in spite of the topic's grimness.
Alice sometimes had a peculiar way of mixing the
King's English with choice bits of underworld and
police vernacular.

"Yes," he said.

"I'm awfully sorry," she answered, her mood and her voice changing. "Please be careful, you and Hank. If a cheap hood is shooting up the streets . . ."

"We'll be careful," he said. "I've got to go now, Alice."

"I leave Hank in capable hands," Alice said, and she hung up without saying goodbye.

Carella grinned and shrugged, and then put the receiver back into the cradle. David Foster, his brown face looking scrubbed and shining, ambled over to the desk. "Afternoon, Steve," he said.

"Hi, Dave. What've you got?"

"Ballistics report on that .45 you brought in last night."

"Any luck?"

"Hasn't been fired since Old King Cole ordered the bowl."

"Well, that narrows it down," Carella said. "Now we've only got the nine million, nine hundred ninety-nine thousand other people in this fair city to contend with."

"I don't like it when cops get killed," Foster said. His brow lowered menacingly, giving him the appearance of a bull ducking his head to charge at the *muleta*. "Mike was my partner. He was a good guy."

"I know."

"I been trying to think who," Foster said. "I got my personal I.B. right up here, and I been leafing through them mug shots one by one." He tapped his temple. "I been turning them over and studying them, and so far I haven't got anything, but give me

time. Somebody musta had it in for Mike, and when
that face falls into place, that guy's gonna wish he
was in Alaska."

"Tell you the truth," Carella said, "I wish I was
there right now."

"Hot, ain't it?" Foster said, classically understating
the temperature and humidity.

"Yeah." From the corner of his eye, Carella saw
Bush walk down the corridor, push through the railing, and sign in. He walked to Carella's desk, pulled
over a swivel chair and plopped into it disconsolately.

"Rough night?" Foster asked, grinning.

"The roughest," Bush said in his quiet voice.

"Clarke was a blank," Carella told him.

"I figured as much. Where do we go from here?"

"That's a good question."

"Coroner's report in yet?"

"No."

"The boys picked up some hoods for question-
ing," Foster said. "We might give them the once
over."

"Where are they? Downstairs?" Carella asked.

"In the Waldorf Suite," Foster said, referring to
the detention cells on the first floor of the building.

"Why don't you call down for them?"

"Sure," Foster said.

"Where's the Skipper?"

"He's over at Homicide North. He's trying to
goose them into some real action on this one."

"You see the paper this morning?" Bush asked.

"No," Carella said.

"Mike made the front page. Have a look." He put

the paper on Carella's desk. Carella held it up so that Foster could see it while he spoke on the phone.

"Shot him in the back," Foster mumbled. "That lousy bastard." He spoke into the phone and then hung up. The men lighted cigarettes, and Bush phoned out for coffee, and then they sat around gassing. The prisoners arrived before the coffee did.

There were two men, both unshaven, both tall, both wearing short-sleeved sports shirts. The physical resemblance ended there. One of the men owned a handsome face, with regular features and white, even teeth. The other man looked as if his face had challenged a concrete mixer and lost. Carella recognized both of them at once. Mentally, he flipped over their cards in the Lousy file.

"Were they picked up together?" he asked the uniformed cop who brought them into the squad room.

"Yeah," the cop said.

"Where?"

"Thirteenth and Shippe. They were sitting in a parked car."

"Any law against that?" the handsome one asked.

"At three in the morning," the uniformed cop added.

"Okay," Carella said. "Thanks."

"What's your name?" Bush asked the handsome one.

"You know my name, cop."

"Say it again. I like the sound."

"I'm tired."

"You're gonna be a lot more tired before this is

finished. Now cut the comedy, and answer the questions. Your name?"

"Terry."

"Terry what?"

"Terry McCarthy. What the hell is this, a joke? You know my name."

"How about your buddy?"

"You know him, too. He's Clarence Kelly."

"What were you doing in that car?" Carella asked.

"Lookin' at dirty pictures," McCarthy said.

"Possession of pornography," Carella said dully. "Take that down, Hank."

"Hey, wait a minute," McCarthy said. "I was only wisecrackin'."

"DON'T WISECRACK ON MY TIME!!" Carella shouted.

"Okay, okay, don't get sore."

"What were you doing in that car?"

"Sitting."

"You always sit in parked cars at three in the A.M.?" Foster asked.

"Sometimes," McCarthy said.

"What else were you doing?"

"Talking."

"What about?"

"Everything."

"Philosophy?" Bush asked.

"Yeah," McCarthy said.

"What'd you decide?"

"We decided it ain't wise to sit in parked cars at three in the morning. There's always some cop who's got to fill his pinch book."

Carella tapped a pencil on the desk. "Don't get me mad, McCarthy," he said. "I just come from six hours sleep, and I don't feel like listening to a vaudeville routine. Did you know Mike Reardon?"

"Who?"

"Mike Reardon. A detective attached to this precinct."

McCarthy shrugged. He turned to Kelly. "We know him, Clarence?"

"Yeah," Clarence said. "Reardon. That rings a bell."

"How big a bell?" Foster asked.

"Just a tiny tinkle so far," Kelly said, and he began laughing. The laugh died when he saw the bulls weren't quite appreciating his humor.

"Did you see him last night?"

"No."

"How do you know?"

"We didn't run across any bulls last night," Kelly said.

"Do you usually?"

"Well, sometimes."

"Were you heeled when they pulled you in?"

"What?"

"Come on," Foster said.

"No."

"We'll check that."

"Yeah, go ahead," McCarthy said. "We didn't even have a water pistol between us."

"What were you doing in the car?"

"I just told you," McCarthy said.

"The story stinks. Try again," Carella answered.

Kelly sighed. McCarthy looked at him.

"Well?" Carella said.

"I was checkin' up on my dame," Kelly said.

"Yeah?" Bush said.

"Truth," Kelly said. "So help me Jesus, may I be struck dead right this goddamn minute."

"What's there to check up on?" Bush asked.

"Well, you know."

"No, I don't know. Tell me."

"I figured she was maybe slippin' around."

"Slipping around with who?" Bush asked.

"Well, that's what I wanted to find out."

"And what were you doing with him, McCarthy?"

"I was helping him check," McCarthy said, smiling.

"Was she?" Bush asked, a bored expression on his face.

"No, I don't think so," Kelly said.

"Don't check again," Bush said. "Next time we're liable to find you with the burglar's tools."

"Burglar's tools!" McCarthy said, shocked.

"Gee, Detective Bush," Kelly said, "you know us better than that."

"Get the hell out of here," Bush said.

"We can go home?"

"You can go to hell, for my part," Bush informed them.

"Here's the coffee," Foster said.

The released prisoners sauntered out of the squad room. The three detectives paid the delivery boy for the coffee and then pulled chairs up to one of the desks.

"I heard a good one last night," Foster said.

"Let's hear it," Carella prompted.

"This guy is a construction worker, you see?"

"Yeah."

"Working up on a girder about sixty floors above the street."

"Yeah?"

"The lunch whistle blows. He knocks off, goes to the end of the girder, sits down, and puts his lunch box on his lap. He opens the box, takes out a sandwich and very carefully unwraps the waxed paper. Then he bites into it. 'Goddamn!' he says, 'peanut butter!' and he throws the sandwich down the sixty floors to the street."

"I don't get it," Bush said, sipping at his coffee.

"I'm not finished yet," Foster said, grinning, hardly able to contain his glee.

"Go ahead," Carella said.

"He reaches into the box," Foster said, "for the next sandwich. He very carefully unwraps the waxed paper. He bites into the sandwich. 'Goddamn!' he says again, 'peanut butter!' and he flings that second sandwich down the sixty floors to the street."

"Yeah," Carella said.

"He opens the third sandwich," Foster said. "This time it's ham. This time he likes it. He eats the sandwich all up."

"This is gonna go on all night," Bush said. "You shoulda stood in bed, Dave."

"No, wait a minute, wait a minute," Foster said. "He opens the fourth sandwich. He bites into it. 'Goddamn!' he says again, 'peanut butter!' and he flings that sandwich too down the sixty floors to the street. Well, there's another construction worker sitting on a girder just a little bit above this fellow. He looks down and says, 'Say, fellow, I've been watching you with them sandwiches.'

" 'So what?' the first guy says.

" 'You married?' the second guy asks.

" 'Yes, I'm married.'

"The second guy shakes his head. 'How long you been married?'

" 'Ten years,' the first guy says.

" 'And your wife still doesn't know what kind of sandwiches you like?'

"The first guy points his finger up at the guy above him and yells, 'Listen, you son of a bitch, leave my wife out of this. I made those goddamn sandwiches myself!' "

Carella burst out laughing, almost choking on his coffee. Bush stared at Foster dead-panned.

"I still don't get it," Bush said. "What's so funny about a guy married ten years whose wife doesn't know what kind of sandwiches he likes? That's not funny. That's a tragedy."

"He made the sandwiches *himself,*" Foster said.

"So then it's a psycho joke. Psycho jokes don't appeal to me. You got to be nuts to appreciate a psycho joke."

"I appreciate it," Carella said.

"So? That proves my point," Bush answered.

"Hank didn't get enough sleep," Carella said to Foster. Foster winked.

"I got plenty of sleep," Bush said.

"Ah-ha," Carella said. "Then that explains it."

"What the hell do you mean by that?" Bush said, annoyed.

"Oh, forget it. Drink your coffee."

"A man doesn't get a joke, right away his sex life gets dragged in. Do I ask you how much sleep you get or don't get?"

"No," Carella said.

"Okay. Okay."

One of the patrolmen walked into the squad room. "Desk sergeant asked me to give you this," he said. "Just came up from Downtown."

"Probably that Coroner's report," Carella said, taking the manila envelope. "Thanks."

The patrolman nodded and went out. Carella opened the envelope.

"Is it?" Foster asked.

"Yeah. Something else, too." He pulled a card from the envelope. "Oh, report on the slugs they dug out of the theatre booth."

"Let's see it," Hank said.

Carella handed him the card.

BULLET

Caliber	Weight	Twist	No. of Grooves
.45	230 grms.	16 L	6
Width of land marks		Width of groove marks	
.071		.158	
Metal Case	Half Metal	Soft Point	
Brass		No	
Deceased		Date	
Michael Reardon		July 24th	
Remarks:			
Remington bullet taken from wooden booth behind body of Michael Reardon.			

"Argh, so what does it tell us?" Bush said, still smarting from the earlier badinage.

"Nothing," Carella answered, "until we get the gun that fired it."

"What about the Coroner's report?" Foster asked. Carella slipped it out of the envelope.

CORONER'S PRELIMINARY AUTOPSY REPORT

MICHAEL REARDON

Male, apparent age 42; chronological age 38. Approximate weight 210 pounds; height 28.9 cm.

Gross Inspection

HEAD: 1.0 x 1.25 cm circular perforation visible 3.1 centimeters laterally to the left of external occipital protuberance (inion). Wound edges slightly inverted. Flame zone and second zone reveal heavy embedding of powder grains. A number 22 catheter inserted through the wound in the occipital region of the skull transverses ventrally and emerges through the right orbit. Point of emergence has left a gaping rough-edged wound measuring 3.7 centimeters in diameter.

There is a second perforation located 6.2 centimeters laterally to the left of the tip of the right mastoid process of the temporal bone, measuring 1.0 x 1.33 centimeters. A number 22 catheter inserted through this second wound passes anteriorly and ventrally and emerges through a perforation measuring approximately 3.5 centimeters in diameter through the right maxilla. The edges of the remaining portion of the right maxilla are splintered.

BODY: Gross inspection of remaining portion of body is negative for demonstrable pathology.

REMARKS: On craniotomy with brain examination, there is evidence of petechiae along course of projectile; small splinters of cranial bone are embedded within the brain substance.

MICROSCOPIC: Examination of brain reveals minute petechiae as well as bone substance within brain matter. Microscopic examination of brain tissue is essentially negative for pathology.

"He did a good job, the bastard," Foster said.

"Yeah," Bush answered.

Carella sighed and looked at his watch. "It's going to be a long night, fellers," he said.

6

He had not seen Teddy Franklin since Mike took the slugs.

Generally, in the course of running down something, he would drop in to see her, spending a few minutes with her before rushing off again. And, of course, he spent all his free time with her because he was in love with the girl.

He had met her less than six months ago, when she'd been working addressing envelopes for a small firm on the fringe of the precinct territory. The firm reported a burglary, and Carella had been assigned to it. He had been taken instantly with her buoyant beauty, asked her out, and that had been the beginning. He had also, in the course of investigation, cracked the burglary—but that didn't seem important now. The important thing now was Teddy. Even the firm had gone the way of most small firms, fading into the abyss of a corporate dissolution, leaving her without a job but with enough saved money to maintain herself for a while. He honestly hoped it would only be for a while, a short while at that. This was the girl he wanted to marry. This was the girl he wanted for his own.

Thinking of her, thinking of the progression of slow traffic lights which kept him from racing to her side, he cursed Ballistics Reports and Coroner's Reports, and people who shot cops in the back of the head, and he cursed the devilish instrument known as the telephone and the fact that the instrument was worthless with a girl like Teddy. He glanced at his watch. It was close to midnight, and she didn't know he was coming, but he'd take the chance, anyway. He wanted to see her.

When he reached her apartment building in Riverhead, he parked the car and locked it. The street was very quiet. The building was old and sedate, covered with lush ivy. A few windows blinked wide-eyed at the stifling heat of the night, but most of the tenants were asleep or trying to sleep. He glanced up at her window, pleased when he saw the light was still burning. Quickly, he mounted the steps, stopping outside her door.

He did not knock.

Knocking was no good with Teddy.

He took the knob in his hand and twisted it back and forth, back and forth. In a few moments, he heard her footsteps, and then the door opened a crack, and then the door opened wide.

She was wearing prisoner pajamas, white-and-black striped cotton top and pants she'd picked up as a gag. Her hair was raven black, and the light in the foyer put a high sheen onto it. He closed the door behind him, and she went instantly into his

arms, and then she moved back from him, and he
marveled at the expressiveness of her eyes and her
mouth. There was joy in her eyes, pure soaring joy.
Her lips parted, edging back over small white teeth,
and then she lifted her face to his, and he took her
kiss, and he felt the warmth of her body beneath the
cotton pajamas.

"Hello," he said, and she kissed the words on his
mouth, and then broke away, holding only his hand,
pulling him into the warmly lit living room.

She held her right index finger alongside her
face, calling for his attention.

"Yes?" he said, and then she shook her head,
changing her mind, wanting him to sit first. She
fluffed a pillow for him, and he sat in the easy chair,
and she perched herself on the arm of the chair and
cocked her head to one side, repeating the extended index finger gesture.

"Go ahead," he said, "I'm listening."

She watched his lips carefully, and then she
smiled. Her index finger dropped. There was a
white tag sewed onto the prisoner pajama top close
to the mound of her left breast. She ran the extended finger across the tag. He looked at it closely.

"I'm not examining your feminine attributes," he
said, smiling, and she shook her head, understanding.
She had inked numbers onto the tag, carrying out the
prison garb motif. He studied the numbers closely.

"My shield numbers," he said, and the smile flow-
ered on her mouth. "You deserve a kiss for that," he
told her.

She shook her head.

"No kiss?"

She shook her head again.

"Why not?"

She opened and closed the fingers on her right hand.

"You want to talk?" he asked.

She nodded.

"What about?"

She left the arm of the chair suddenly. He watched her walking across the room, his eyes inadvertently following the swing of her small, rounded backside. She went to an end table and picked up a newspaper. She carried it back to him and then pointed to the picture of Mike Reardon on page one, his brains spilling out onto the sidewalk.

"Yeah," he said dully.

There was sadness on her face now, an exaggerated sadness because Teddy could not give tongue to words, Teddy could neither hear words, and so her face was her speaking tool, and she spoke in exaggerated syllables, even to Carella, who understood the slightest nuance of expression in her eyes or on her mouth. But the exaggeration did not lie, for there was genuineness to the grief she felt. She had never met Mike Reardon, but Carella had talked of him often, and she felt that she knew him well.

She raised her eyebrows and spread her hands simultaneously, asking Carella "Who?" and Carella, understanding instantly, said, "We don't know yet. That's why I haven't been around. We've been working on it." He saw puzzlement in her eyes. "Am I going too fast for you?" he asked.

She shook her head.

"What then? What's the matter?"

She threw herself into his arms and she was weeping suddenly and fiercely, and he said, "Hey, hey, come on, now," and then realized she could not read his lips because her head was buried in his shoulder. He lifted her chin.

"You're getting my shirt wet," he said.

She nodded, trying to hold back the tears.

"What's the matter?"

She lifted her hand slowly, and she touched his cheek gently, so gently that it felt like the passing of a mild breeze, and then her fingers touched his lips and lingered there, caressing them.

"You're worried about me?"

She nodded.

"There's nothing to worry about."

She tossed her hair at the first page of the newspaper again.

"That was probably some crackpot," Carella said.

She lifted her face, and her eyes met his fully, wide and brown, still moist from the tears.

"I'll be careful," he said. "Do you love me?"

She nodded, and then ducked her head.

"What's the matter?"

She shrugged and smiled, an embarrassed, shy smile.

"You missed me?"

She nodded again.

"I missed you, too."

She lifted her head again, and there was something else in her eyes this time, a challenge to him to read her eyes correctly this time, because she had truly missed him but he had not uncovered the subtlety of her meaning as yet. He studied her eyes, and then he knew what she was saying, and he said only, "Oh."

She knew that he knew then, and she cocked one eyebrow saucily and slowly gave one exaggerated nod of her head, repeating his "oh," soundlessly rounding her lips.

"You're just a fleshpot," he said jokingly.

She nodded.

"You only love me because I have a clean, strong, young body."

She nodded.

"Will you marry me?"

She nodded.

"I've only asked you about a dozen times so far."

She shrugged and nodded, enjoying herself immensely.

"When?"

She pointed at him.

"All right, I'll set the date. I'm getting my vacation in August. I'll marry you then, okay?"

She sat perfectly still, staring at him.

"I mean it."

She seemed ready to cry again. He took her in his arms and said, "I mean it, Teddy. Teddy, darling, I mean it. Don't be silly about this, Teddy, because I honestly, truly mean it. I love you, and I want to marry you, and I've wanted to marry you for a long, long time now, and if I have to keep asking you, I'll go nuts. I love you just the way you are, I wouldn't change any of you, darling, so don't get silly, please don't get silly again. It . . . it doesn't matter to me, Teddy. Little Teddy, little Theodora, it doesn't matter to me, can you understand that? You're *more* than any other woman, so much more, so please marry me."

She looked up at him, wishing she could speak because she could not trust her eyes now, wondering why someone as beautiful as Steve Carella, as wonderful as Steve Carella, as brave and as strong and as marvelous as Steve Carella would want to marry a girl like her, a girl who could never say, "I love you, darling. I adore you." But he had asked her again, and now, close in the circle of his arms, now she could believe that it didn't really matter to him, that to him she was as whole as any woman, "more than any other woman," he had said.

"Okay?" he asked. "Will you let me make you honest?"

She nodded. The nod was a very small one.

"You mean it this time?"

She did not nod again. She lifted her mouth, and she put her answer into her lips, and his arms tightened around her, and she knew that he understood her. She broke away from him, and he said, "Hey!" but she trotted away from his reach and went to the kitchen.

When she brought back the champagne, he said, "I'll be damned!"

She sighed, agreeing that he undoubtedly would be damned, and he slapped her playfully on the fanny.

She handed him the bottle, did a deep curtsy which was ludicrous in the prisoner pajamas and then sat on the floor cross-legged while he struggled with the cork.

The champagne exploded with an enormous pop, and though she did not hear the sound, she saw the cork leave the neck of the bottle and ricochet off the ceiling, and she saw the bubbly white fluid over-spilling the lip and running over his hands.

She began to clap, and then she got to her feet and went for glasses, and he poured first a little of the wine into his, saying, "That's the way it's done, you know. It's supposed to take off the skim and the bugs and everything," and then filling her glass, and then going back to pour his to the brim.

"To us," he toasted.

She opened her arms slowly, wider and wider and wider.

"A long, long, happy love," he supplied.

She nodded happily.

"And our marriage in August." They clinked glasses, and then sipped at the wine, and she opened her eyes wide in pleasure and cocked her head appreciatively.

"Are you happy?" he asked.

Yes, her eyes said, yes, yes.

"Did you mean what you said before?"

She raised one brow inquisitively.

"About . . . missing me?"

Yes, yes, yes, yes, her eyes said.

"You're beautiful."

She curtsied again.

"Everything about you. I love you, Teddy. Jesus, how I love you."

She put down the wineglass and then took his hand. She kissed the palm of the hand, and the back, and then she led him into the bedroom, and she unbuttoned his shirt and pulled it out of his trousers, her hands moving gently. He lay down on the bed, and she turned off the light and then, unselfconsciously, unembarrassedly, she took off the pajamas and went to him.

And while they made gentle love in a small room in a big apartment house, a man named David Foster walked toward his own apartment, an apartment he shared with his mother.

And while their love grew fierce and then gentle again, a man named David Foster thought about his partner Mike Reardon, and so immersed in his thoughts was he that he did not hear the footsteps behind him, and when he finally did hear them, it was too late.

He started to turn, but a .45 automatic spat orange flame into the night, once, twice, again, again, and David Foster clutched at his chest, and the red blood burst through his brown fingers, and then he hit the concrete—dead.

7

There is not much you can say to a man's mother when the man is dead. There is not much you can say at all.

Carella sat in the doilied easy chair and looked across at Mrs. Foster. The early afternoon sunlight seeped through the drawn blinds in the small, neat living room, narrow razor-edge bands of brilliance against the cool dimness. The heat in the streets was still insufferable, and he was thankful for the cool living room, but his topic was death, and he would have preferred the heat.

Mrs. Foster was a small, dried-up woman. Her face was wrinkled and seamed, as brown as David's had been. She sat hunched in the chair, a small withered woman with a withered face and withered hands, and he thought, *A strong wind would blow her away, poor woman,* and he watched the grief that lay quietly contained behind the expressionless withered face.

"David was a good boy," she said. Her voice was hollow, a narrow sepulchral voice. He had come to talk of death, and now he could smell death on this woman, could hear death in the creak of her voice, and he thought it strange that David Foster, her son, who was alive and strong and young several hours ago was now dead—and his mother, who had probably longed for the peaceful sleep of death many a time, was alive and talking to Carella.

"Always a good boy. You raise 'em in a neighborhood like this one," Mrs. Foster said, "and you fear for how they'll turn out. My husband was a good worker, but he died young, and it wasn't always easy to see that David wasn't needing. But he was a good boy, always. He would come home and tell me what the other boys were doing, the stealing and all the things they were doing, and I knew he was all right."

"Yes, Mrs. Foster," Carella said.

"And they all liked him around here, too," Mrs. Foster went on, shaking her head. "All the boys he grew up with, and all the old folks, too. The people around here, Mr. Carella, they don't take much to cops. But they liked my David because he grew up among them, and he was a part of them, and I guess they were sort of proud of him, the way I was proud."

"We were all proud of him, Mrs. Foster," Carella said.

"He was a good cop, wasn't he?"

"Yes, he was a fine cop."

"Then why would anyone want to kill him?" Mrs. Foster asked. "Oh, I knew his job was a dangerous one, yes, but this is different, this is senseless. He wasn't even on duty. He was coming home. Who would want to shoot my boy, Mr. Carella? Who would want to shoot my boy?"

"That's what I wanted to talk to you about, Mrs. Foster. I hope you don't mind if I ask a few questions."

"If it'll help you find the man who killed David, I'll answer questions all day for you."

"Did he ever talk about his work?"

"Yes, he did. He always told me what happened around the precinct, what you were working on. He told me about his partner being killed, and he told me he was leafing through pictures in his mind, just waiting until he hit the right one."

"Did he say anything else about the pictures? Did he say he suspected anyone?"

"No."

"Mrs. Foster, what about his friends?"

"Everyone was his friend."

"Did he have an address book or anything in which their names might be listed?"

"I don't think he had an address book, but there's a pad near the telephone he always used."

"May I have that before I leave?"

"Certainly."

"Did he have a sweetheart?"

"No, not anyone steady. He went out with a lot of different girls."

"Did he keep a diary?"

"No."

"Does he have a photograph collection?"

"Yes, he liked music a lot. He was always playing his records whenever he . . ."

"No, not phonograph. Photograph."

"Oh. No. He carried a few pictures in his wallet, but that's all."

"Did he ever tell you where he went on his free time?"

"Oh, lots of different places. He liked the theatre a lot. The stage, I mean. He went often."

"These boyhood friends of his. Did he pal around with them much?"

"No, I don't think so."

"Did he drink?"

"Not heavily."

"I mean, would you know whether or not he frequented any of the bars in the neighborhood? Social drinking, of course."

"I don't know."

"Had he received any threatening letters or notes that you know of?"

"He never mentioned any."

"Ever behave peculiarly on the telephone?"

"Peculiarly? What do you mean?"

"Well, as if he were trying to hide something from you. Or as if he were worried . . . anything like that. I'm thinking of threatening calls, Mrs. Foster."

"No, I don't ever remember him acting strange on the phone."

"I see. Well . . ." Carella consulted his notes. "I guess that's about it. I want to get going, Mrs. Foster, because there's a lot of work to do. If you could get me that telephone pad . . ."

"Yes, of course." She rose, and he watched her slight body as she moved out of the cool living room into one of the bedrooms. When she returned, she handed him the pad and said, "Keep it as long as you like."

"Thank you. Mrs. Foster, please know that we all share your sorrow," he said lamely.

"Find my boy's killer," Mrs. Foster said. She extended one of her withered hands and took his hand in a strong, firm grip, and he marveled at the strength of the grip, and at the strength in her eyes and on her face. Only when he was in the hallway, with the door locked behind him, did he hear the gentle sobs that came from within the apartment.

He went downstairs and out to the car. When he reached the car, he took off his jacket, wiped his face, and then sat behind the wheel to study his worksheet:

STATEMENT OF EYEWITNESSES: None.

MOTIVE: Revenge? Con? Nut? Tie-in with Mike? Check Ballistics report.

NUMBER OF MURDERERS: Two? One Mike, one David. Or tie-in? B.R. again.

WEAPONS: .45 automatic.

ROUTE OF MURDERER: ?

DIARIES, JOURNALS, LETTERS, ADDRESSES, TELEPHONE NUMBERS, PHOTOGRAPHS: Check with David's mthr.

ASSOCIATES, RELATIVES, SWEETHEARTS, ENEMIES, ETC: DITTO.

PLACES FREQUENTED, HANG-OUTS: Ditto.

HABITS: Ditto.

TRACES AND CLUES FOUND ON THE SCENE: Heel

print in dog feces. At Lab now. Four shells.
Two bullets. Ditto.
FINGERPRINTS FOUND: None.

Carella scratched his head, sighed against the
heat, and then headed back for the precinct house
to see if the new Ballistics report had come in yet.

The widow of Michael Reardon was a full-breasted
woman in her late thirties. She had dark hair and
green eyes, and an Irish nose spattered with a cliché-
ful of freckles. She had a face for merry-go-rounds
and roller-coaster rides, a face that could split in
laughter and girlish glee when water was splashed
on her at the seashore. She was a girl who could get
drunk sniffing the vermouth cork before it was
passed over a martini. She was a girl who went to
church on Sundays, a girl who'd belonged to the
Newman Club when she was younger, a girl who was
a virgin two days after Mike had taken her for his
bride. She had good legs, very white, and a good
body, and her name was May.

She was dressed in black on the hot afternoon of
July 25th, and her feet were planted firmly on the
floor before her, and her hands were folded in her
lap, and there was no laughter on the face made for
roller-coaster rides.

"I haven't told the children yet," she said to Bush.
"The children don't know. How can I tell them?
What can I say?"

"It's a rough thing," Bush said in his quiet voice.
His scalp felt sticky and moist. He needed a hair-

cut, and his wild red hair was shrieking against the
heat.

"Yes," May said. "Can I get you a beer or something? It's very hot. Mike used to take a beer when
he got home. No matter what time it was, he always
took a beer. He was a very well-ordered person. I
mean, he did things carefully and on schedule. I
think he wouldn't have been able to sleep if he
didn't have that glass of beer when he got home."

"Did he ever stop in the neighborhood bars?"

"No. He always drank here, in the house. And
never whiskey. Only one or two glasses of beer."

Mike Reardon, Bush thought. *He used to be a cop and
a friend. Now he's a victim and a corpse, and I ask questions about him.*

"We were supposed to get an air-conditioning
unit," May said. "At least, we talked about it. This
apartment gets awfully hot. That's because we're so
close to the building next door."

"Yes," Bush said. "Mrs. Reardon, did Mike have
any enemies that you know of? I mean, people he
knew outside his line of duty?"

"No, I don't think so. Mike was a very easygoing
sort. Well, you worked with him. You know."

"Can you tell me what happened the night he was
killed? Before he left the house?"

"I was sleeping when he left. Whenever he had
the twelve-to-eight tour, we argued about whether
we should try to get any sleep before he went in."

"Argued?"

"Well, you know, we discussed it. Mike preferred
staying up, but I have two children, and I'm beat

when it hits ten o'clock. So he usually compromised on those nights, and we both got to bed early—at about nine, I suppose."

"Were you asleep when he left?"

"Yes. But I woke up just before he went out."

"Did he say anything to you? Anything that might indicate he was worried about an ambush? Had he received a threat or anything?"

"No." May Reardon glanced at her watch. "I have to be leaving soon, Detective Bush. I have an appointment at the funeral parlor. I wanted to ask you about that. I know you're doing tests on . . . on the body and all . . . but the family . . . Well, the family is kind of old-fashioned and we want to . . . we want to make arrangements. Do you have any idea when . . . when you'll be finished with him?"

"Soon, Mrs. Reardon. We don't want to miss any bets. A careful autopsy may put us closer to finding his killer."

"Yes, I know. I didn't want you to think . . . it's just the family. They ask questions. They don't understand. They don't know what it means to have him gone, to wake up in the morning and not . . . not have him here." She bit her lip and turned her face from Bush. "Forgive me. Mike wouldn't . . . wouldn't like this. Mike wouldn't want me to . . ." She shook her head and swallowed heavily. Bush watched her, feeling sudden empathy for this woman who was Wife, feeling sudden compassion for all women everywhere who had ever had their men torn from them by violence. His thoughts wandered to Alice, and he wondered idly how she would feel if he stopped a bullet, and then he put the thought out of his mind. It wasn't good to think things like that. Not these days. Not after two in a row. Jesus, was it possible there was a nut loose? Somebody who'd marked the whole goddamn precinct as his special target?

Yes, it was possible.

It was very damn possible, and so it wasn't good to think about things like Alice's reaction to his own death. You thought about things like that, and they consumed your mind, and then when you needed a clear mind which could react quickly to possible danger, you didn't have it. And that's when you were up the creek without a paddle.

What had Mike Reardon been thinking of when he'd been gunned down?

What had been in the mind of David Foster when the four slugs ripped into his body?

Of course, it was possible the two deaths were un-related. Possible, but not very probable. The m.o. was remarkably similar, and once the Ballistics re-port came through they'd know for sure whether they were dealing with one man or two.

Bush's money was on the one-man possibility.

"If there's anything else you want to ask me," May said. She had pulled herself together now, and she faced him squarely, her face white, her eyes large.

"If you'll just collect any address books, pho-tographs, telephone numbers, newspaper clippings he may have saved, anything that may give us a lead onto his friends or even his relatives, I'd be much obliged."

"Yes, I can do that," May said.

"And you can't remember anything unusual that may have some bearing on this, is that right?"

"No, I can't. Detective Bush, what am I going to tell the kids? I sent them off to a movie. I told them their daddy was out on a plant. But how long can I keep it from them? How do you tell a pair of kids that their father is dead? Oh God, what am I going to do?"

Bush remained silent. In a little while, May Reardon went for the stuff he wanted.

At 3:42 P.M. on July 25th, the Ballistics report reached Carella's desk. The shells and bullets found at the scene of Mike Reardon's death had been put beneath the comparison microscope together with the shells and bullets used in the killing of David Foster.

The Ballistics report stated that the same weapon had been used in both murders.

8

On the night that David Foster was killed, a care-less mongrel searching for food in garbage cans, had paused long enough to sully the sidewalk of the city. The dog had been careless, to be sure, and a human being had been just as careless, and there was a portion of a heelprint for the Lab boys to work over, solely because of this combined record of care-lessness. The Lab boys turned to with something akin to distaste.

The heelprint was instantly photographed, not because the boys liked to play with cameras, but simply because they knew accidents frequently oc-curred in the making of a cast. The heelprint was placed on a black-stained cardboard scale, marked off in inches. The camera, supported above the print by a reversible tripod, the lens parallel to the print to avoid any false perspectives, clicked merrily away. Satisfied that the heelprint was now preserved for posterity—photographically, at least—the Lab boys turned to the less antiseptic task of making the cast.

One of the boys filled a rubber cup with half a pint of water. Then he spread plaster of Paris over the water, taking care not to stir it, allowing it to sink to the bottom of its own volition. He kept adding plaster of Paris until the water couldn't absorb anymore of it, until he'd dumped about ten ounces of it into the cup. Then he brought the cup to one of the other boys who was preparing the print to take the mixture.

Because the print was in a soft material, it was sprayed first with shellac and then with a thin coat of oil. The plaster of Paris mixture was stirred and then carefully applied to the prepared print. It was applied with a spoon in small portions. When the print was covered to a thickness of about one-third of an inch, the boys spread pieces of twine and sticks onto the plaster to reinforce it, taking care that the debris did not touch the bottom of the print and destroy its details. They then applied another coat of plaster to the print, and allowed the cast to harden. From time to time, they touched the plaster, feeling for warmth, knowing that warmth meant the cast was hardening.

Since there was only one print, and since it was not even a full print, and since it was impossible to get a Walking Picture from this single print, and since the formula $H\dfrac{r}{l}$ BS $\dfrac{ra\ rv\ raa}{la\ lv\ laa} \cdot \dfrac{ll\ lb}{rl\ rb}$ X, a formula designed to give the complete picture of a man's walk in terms of step length, breadth of step, length of left foot, right foot, greatest width of left foot, right foot, wear on heel and sole—since the formula could not be applied to a single print, the Lab boys did all they could with what they had.

And they decided, after careful study, that the heel was badly worn on the outside edge, a peculiarity which told them the man belonging to that heel undoubtedly walked with a somewhat ducklike waddle. They also decided that the heel was not the original heel of the shoe, that it was a rubber heel which had been put on during a repair job, and that the third nail from the shank side of the heel, on the left, had been bent when applying the new heel.

And—quite coincidentally *if* the heelprint happened to have been left by the murderer—the heel bore the clearly stamped trade name "O'Sullivan," and everyone knows that O'Sullivan is America's Number One Heel.

The joke was an old one. The Lab boys hardly laughed at all.

The newspapers were not laughing very much, either.

The newspapers were taking this business of cop-killing quite seriously. Two morning tabloids, showing remarkable versatility in headlining the same incident, respectively reported the death of David Foster with the words SECOND COP SLAIN and KILLER SLAYS 2ND COP.

The afternoon tabloid, a newspaper hard-pressed to keep up with the circulation of the morning

sheets, boldly announced KILLER ROAMS
STREETS. And then, because this particular newspaper was vying for circulation, and because this
particular newspaper made it a point to "expose"
anything which happened to be in the public's eye
at the moment—anything from Daniel Boone to
long winter underwear, anything which gave them a
free circulation ride on the then-popular bandwag-
on—their front page carried a red banner that day,
and the red banner shouted "The Police Jungle—
What Goes On In Our Precincts" and then in small-
eɪ white type against the red, "See Murray
Schneider, p. 4."

And anyone who had the guts to wade through
the first three pages of cheesecake and chest-
thumping liberalism, discovered on page four that
Murray Schneider blamed the deaths of Mike Reardon and David Foster upon "the graft-loaded cor-
ruptness of our filth-ridden Gestapo."

In the graft-loaded squad room of the corrupt
87th Precinct, two detectives named Steve Carella
and Hank Bush stood behind a filth-ridden desk
and pored over several cards their equally corrupt fellow-officers had dug from the Convictions
file.

"Try this for size," Bush said.

"I'm listening," Carella said.

"Some punk gets pinched by Mike and Dave,
right?"

"Right."

"The judge throws the book at him, and he gets

room and board from the State for the next five or ten years. Okay?"

"Okay."

"Then he gets out. He's had a lot of time to mull this over, a lot of time to build up his original peeve into a big hate. The one thing in his mind is to get Mike and Dave. So he goes out for them. He gets Mike first, and then he tries to get Dave quick, before this hate of his cools down. Wham, he gets Dave, too."

"It reads good," Carella said.

"That's why I don't buy this Flannagan punk."

"Why not?"

"Take a look at the card. Burglary, possession of burglary tools, a rape away back in '47. Mike and Dave got him on the last burglary pinch. This was the first time he got convicted, and he drew ten, just got out last month on parole after doing five years."

"So?"

"So I don't figure a guy with a big hate is going to be good enough to cut ten years to five. Besides, Flannagan never carried a gun all the while he was working. He was a gent."

"Guns are easy to come by."

"Sure. But I don't figure him for our man."

"I'd like to check him out, anyway," Carella said.

"Okay, but I want to check this other guy out first. Ordiz. Luis 'Dizzy' Ordiz. Take a look at the card."

			NAME OF PRISONER	
Precinct		(Surname)	(First Name and Init.)	
87th		ORDIZ	LUIS "DIZZY"	

Date & Time of Arrest		Address of Prisoner	
May 2, 1952 7:00 PM		635 6th St. South	

Sex	Color	Date of Birth Mo. Day Year	Place of Birth	~~Alien~~ Citizen
M	Whte	8 12 1912	San Juan, Puerto Rico	

Social Condition	Read and Write	Occupation	Employed
Married (Single)	Yes (No)	Dishwasher	Yes (No)

Charge	Specific Offense	Date-Time Occurrence
Violation PL 1751 Subdiv. 1	Poss. of nar- cotics with intent to sell.	5/2/52 7:00 PM

Pct. Complaint No.	Place of Occurrence	Precinct
33A-411		
D.B. Complaint No.	635 6th St.	
DD 179-52	South	87th
Name of Complainant	Address of Complainant	

Arresting Officer(s) (Name-s)	Michael Reardon & David Foster
(Rank) Det. 3rd & Det. 2nd Gr.	(Command) Det. Bureau

	Authority		
(Pickup)	Complaint	Warrant	F.O.A.

Action of Court
Sentenced four years at state penitentiary, Ossining, New York

Date	Judge	Court
7/6/52	Fields	

Carella pulled the conviction card closer. The card was a 4 x 6 white rectangle, divided into printed rectangles of various sizes and shapes.

"A hophead," Carella said.

"Yeah. Figure the hate a hophead can build in four years' time."

"He went the distance?"

"Got out the beginning of the month," Bush said. "Cold turkey all that time. This don't build brotherly love for the cops who made the nab."

"No, it doesn't."

"Figure this, too. Take a look at his record. He was picked up in '51 on a dis cond charge. This was before he got on the junk, allegedly. But he was carrying a .45. The gun had a busted hammer, but it was still a .45. Go back to '49. Again, dis cond, fighting in a bar. Had a .45 on him, no busted hammer this time. He got off lucky that time. Suspended sentence."

"Seems to favor .45's."

"Like the guy who killed Mike and Dave. What do you say?"

"I say we take a look. Where is he?"

Bush shrugged. "Your guess is as good as mine."

Danny Gimp was a man who'd had polio when he was a child. He was lucky in that it had not truly crippled him. He had come out of the disease with only a slight limp, and a nickname which would last him the rest of his life. His real surname was Nelson, but very few people knew that, and he was referred to in the neighborhood as Danny Gimp. Even his letters came addressed that way.

Danny was fifty-four years old, but it was impossible to judge his age from his face or his body. He was very small, small all over, his bones, his features, his eyes, his stature. He moved with the loose-hipped walk of an adolescent, and his voice was high and reedy, and his face bore hardly any wrinkles or other telltale signs of age.

Danny Gimp was a stool pigeon.

He was a very valuable man, and the men of the 87th Precinct called him in regularly, and Danny was always ready to comply—whenever he could. It was a rare occasion when Danny could not supply the piece of information the bulls were looking for. On these occasions, there were other stoolies to talk to. Somewhere, somebody had the goods. It was simply a question of finding the right man at the right time.

Danny could usually be found in the third booth on the right-hand side of a bar named *Andy's Pub*. He was not an alcoholic, nor did he even drink to excess. He simply used the bar as a sort of office. It was cheaper than paying rent someplace downtown, and it had the added attraction of a phone booth which he used regularly. The bar, too, was a good place to listen—and listening was one-half of Danny's business. The other half was talking.

He sat opposite Carella and Bush, and first he listened.

Then he talked.

"Dizzy Ordiz," he said. "Yeah, yeah."

"You know where he is?"

"What'd he do?"

"We don't know."

"Last I heard, he was on the state."

"He got out at the beginning of the month."

"Parole?"

"No."

"Ordiz, Ordiz. Oh, yeah. He's a junkie."

"That's right."

"Should be easy to locate. What'd he do?"

"Maybe nothing," Bush said. "Maybe a hell of a lot."

"Oh, you thinking of these cop kills?" Danny asked.

Bush shrugged.

"Not Ordiz. You're barkin' up the wrong tree."

"What makes you say so?"

Danny sipped at his beer, and then glanced up at the rotating fan. "You'd never know there was a fan going in this dump, would you? Jesus, this heat don't break soon, I'm headin' for Canada. I got a friend up there. Quebec. You ever been to Quebec?"

"No," Bush said.

"Nice there. Cool."

"What about Ordiz?"

"Take him with me, he wants to come," Danny said, and then he began laughing at his own joke.

"He's cute today," Carella said.

"I'm cute all the time," Danny said. "I got more dames lined up outside my room than you can count on an abacus. I'm the cutest."

"We didn't know you was pimping," Bush said.

"I ain't. This is all for love."

"How much love you got for Ordiz?"

"Don't know him from a hole in the wall. Don't care to, either. Hopheads make me puke."

"Okay, then where is he?"

"I don't know yet. Give me some time."

"How much time?"

"Hour, two hours. Junkies are easy to trace. Talk to a few pushers, zing, you're in. He got out the beginning of the month, huh? That means he's back on it strong by now. This should be a cinch."

"He may have kicked it," Carella said. "It may not be such a cinch."

"They never kick it," Danny said. "Don't pay attention to fairy tales. He was probably gettin' the stuff sneaked in even up the river. I'll find him. But if you think he knocked off your buddies, you're wrong."

"Why?"

"I seen this jerk around. He's a nowhere. A real *trombenik*, if you dig foreign. He don't know enough to come in out of an atom bomb attack. He got one big thing in his life. Horse. That's Ordiz. He lives for the White God. Only thing on his mind."

"Reardon and Foster sent him away," Carella said.

"So what? You think a junkie bears a grudge? All part of the game. He ain't got time for grudges. He only got time for meetin' his pusher and makin' the buy. This guy Ordiz, he was always half-blind on the stuff. He couldn't see straight enough to shoot off his own big toe. So he's gonna cool two cops? Don't be ridic."

"We'd like to see him anyway," Bush said.

"Sure. Do I tell you how to run Headquarters? Am I the commissioner? But this guy is from Squaresville, fellas, I'm telling you. He wouldn't know a .45 from a cement mixer."

"He's owned a few in his life," Carella said.

"Playing with them, playing with them. If one of them things ever went off within a hundred yards of him, he'd have diarrhea for a week. Take it from me, he don't care about nothin' but heroin. Listen, they don't call him Dizzy for nothin'. He's dizzy. He's got butterflies up here. He chases them away with H."

"I don't trust junkies," Bush said.

"Neither do I," Danny answered. "But this guy ain't a killer, take it from me. He don't even know how to kill time."

"Do us a favor," Carella said.

"Sure."

"Find him for us. You know our number."

"Sure. I'll buzz you in an hour or so. This is gonna be a cinch. Hopheads are a cinch."

9

The heat on that July 26th reached a high of 95.6 at twelve noon. At the precinct house, two fans circulated the soggy air that crawled past the open windows and the grilles behind them. Everything in the Detective Squad Room seemed to wilt under the steady, malignant pressure of the heat. Only the file cabinets and the desks stood at strict attention. Reports, file cards, carbon paper, envelopes, memos, all of these were damp and sticky to the touch, clinging to wherever they were dropped, clinging with a moist limpidity.

The men in the squad room worked in their shirt-sleeves. Their shirts were stained with perspiration, large dark amoeba blots which nibbled at the cloth, spreading from beneath the armpits, spreading from the hollow of the spinal column. The fans did not help the heat at all. The fans circulated the suffocating breath of the city, and the men sucked in the breath and typed up their reports in triplicate, and checked their worksheets, and dreamt of summers in the White Mountains, or summers in Atlantic City with the ocean slapping their faces. They called complainants, and they called suspects, and their hands sweated on the black plastic of the phone, and they could feel Heat like a living thing which invaded their bodies and seared them with a million white-hot daggers.

Lieutenant Byrnes was as hot as any man in the squad room. His office was just to the left of the slatted dividing railing, and it had a large corner window, but the window was wide open and not a breath of a breeze came through it. The reporter sitting opposite him looked cool. The reporter's name was Savage, and the reporter was wearing a blue seersucker suit and a dark blue Panama, and the reporter was smoking a cigarette and casually puffing the smoke up at the ceiling where the heat held it in a solid blue-grey mass.

"There's nothing more I can tell you," Byrnes said. The reporter annoyed him immensely. He did not for a moment believe that any man on this earth had been born with a name like "Savage." He further did not believe that any man on this earth, on this day, could actually be as cool as Savage pretended he was.

"Nothing more, Lieutenant?" Savage asked, his voice very soft. He was a handsome man with close-cropped blond hair and a straight, almost-feminine nose. His eyes were grey, cool. Cool.

"Nothing," the lieutenant said. "What the hell did you expect? If we knew who did it, we'd have him in here, don't you think?"

"I should imagine so," Savage said. "Suspects?"

"We're working on it."

"Suspects?" Savage repeated.

"A few. The suspects are our business. You splash them on your front page, and they'll head for Europe."

"Think a kid did it?"

"What do you mean, a kid?"

"A teenager."

"Anybody could've done it," Byrnes said. "For all I know, *you* did it."

Savage smiled, exposing bright white teeth. "Lots of teenage gangs in this precinct, aren't there?"

"We've got the gangs under control. This precinct isn't the garden spot of the city, Savage, but we like to feel we're doing the best job possible here. Now I realize your newspaper may take offense at that, but we really try, Savage, we honestly try to do our little jobs."

"Do I detect sarcasm in your voice, Lieutenant?" Savage asked.

"Sarcasm is a weapon of the intellectual, Savage. Everybody, especially your newspaper, knows that cops are just stupid, plodding beasts of burden."

"My paper never said that, Lieutenant."

"No?" Byrnes shrugged. "Well, you can use it in tomorrow's edition."

"We're trying to help," Savage said. "We don't like cops getting killed anymore than you do." Savage paused. "What about the teenage gang idea?"

"We haven't even considered it. This isn't the way those gangs operate. Why the hell do you guys try to pin everything that happens in this city on the teenagers? My son is a teenager, and he doesn't go around killing cops."

"That's encouraging," Savage said.

"The gang phenomenon is a peculiar one to understand," Byrnes said. "I'm not saying we've got it licked, but we do have it under control. If we've stopped the street rumbles, and the knifings and shootings, then the gangs have become nothing more than social clubs. As long as they stay that way, I'm happy."

"Your outlook is a strangely optimistic one," Savage said coolly. "My newspaper doesn't happen to believe the street rumbles have stopped. My newspaper is of the opinion that the death of those two cops may be traced directly to these 'social clubs.'"

"Yeah?"

"Yeah."

"So what the hell do you want me to do about it? Round up every kid in the city and shake him down? So your goddamn newspaper can sell another million copies?"

"No. But we're going ahead with our own investigation. And if we crack this, it won't make the 87th Precinct look too good."

"It won't make Homicide North look too good, either. And it won't make the Police Commissioner look good. It'll make everybody in the department look like amateurs as contrasted with the supersleuths of your newspaper."

"Yes, it might," Savage agreed.

"I have a few words of advice for you, Savage."

"Yes?"

"The kids around here don't like questions asked. You're not dealing with Snob Hill teenagers who tie on a doozy by drinking a few cans of beer. You're dealing with kids whose code is entirely different from yours or mine. Don't get yourself killed."

"I won't," Savage said, smiling resplendently.

"And one other thing."

"Yes?"

"Don't foul up my precinct. I got enough headaches without you and your half-assed reporters stirring up more trouble."

"What's more important to you, Lieutenant?" Savage asked. "My not fouling up your precinct—or my not getting killed?"

Byrnes smiled and then began filling his pipe. "They both amount to about the same thing," he said.

The call from Danny Gimp came in fifty minutes. The desk sergeant took the call, and then plugged it in to Carella's line.

"87th Detective Squad," he said. "Carella here."

"Danny Gimp."

"Hello, Danny, what've you got?"

"I found Ordiz."

"Where?"

"This a favor, or business?" Danny asked.

"Business," Carella said tersely. "Where do I meet you?"

"You know Jenny's?"

"You kidding?"

"I'm serious."

"If Ordiz is a junkie, what's he doing on Whore Street?"

"He's blind in some broad's pad. You're lucky you get a few mumbles out of him."

"Whose pad?"

"That's what we meet for, Steve. No?"

"Call me 'Steve' face-to-face, and you'll lose some teeth, pal," Carella said.

"Okay, *Detective* Carella. You want this dope, I'll be in Jenny's in five minutes. Bring some loot."

"Is Ordiz heeled?"

"He may be."

"I'll see you," Carella said.

La Vía de Putas was a street which ran north and south for a total of three blocks. The Indians probably had their name for it, and the tepees that lined the path in those rich days of beaver pelts and painted beads most likely did a thriving business even then. As the Indians retreated to their happy hunting grounds and the well-worn paths turned to paved roads, the tepees gave way to apartment buildings, and the practitioners of the world's oldest profession claimed the plush-lined cubbyholes as their own. There was a time when the street was called *Piazza Putana* by the Italian immigrants, and *The Hussy Hole* by the Irish immigrants. With the Puerto Rican influx, the street had changed its language—but not its sole source of income. The Puerto Ricans referred to it as *La Vía de Putas*. The cops called it "Whore Street." In any language, you paid your money, and you took your choice.

The gals who ran the sex emporiums called them-

selves Mama-this or Mama-that. Mama Theresa's was
the best-known joint on the Street. Mama Carmen's
was the filthiest. Mama Luz's had been raided by the
cops sixteen times because of some of the things
that went on behind its crumbling brick facade. The
cops were not above visiting any of the various
Mamas on social calls, too. The business calls included occasional raids and occasional rake-offs.
The raids were interesting sometimes, but they were
usually conducted by members of the Vice Squad
who were unfamiliar with the working arrangements
some of the 87th Precinct cops had going with the
madams. Nothing can screw up a good deal like an
ignorant cop.

Carella, perhaps, was an ignorant cop. Or an honest one, depending how you looked at it. He met
Danny Gimp at Jenny's, which was a small cafe on
the corner of Whore Street, a cafe which allegedly
served old world absinthe, complete with worm-
wood and water to mix the stuff in. No old-world absinthe drinker had ever been fooled by Jenny's stuff,
but the cafe still served as a sort of no-man's-land between the respectable workaday world of the prole-
tariat, and the sinful shaded halls of the brothels. A
man could hang his hat in Jenny's, and a man could
have a drink there, and a man could pretend he was
on a fraternity outing there, and with the third
drink, he was ready to rationalize what he was about
to do. Jenny's was something necessary to the operation of the Street. Jenny's, to stretch a point, served
the same purpose as the shower stall does in a honeymoon suite.

On July 26th, with the heat baking the black paint that covered the lower half of Jenny's front window—a window which had been smashed in some dozen times since the establishment was founded—Carella and Danny were not interested in the Crossing-the-Social-Barrier aspects of Jenny's bistro. They were interested in a man named Luis "Dizzy" Ordiz, who may or may not have pumped a total of six bullets into a total of two cops. Bush was out checking on the burglar named Flannagan. Carella had come down in a squad car driven by a young rookie named Kling. The squad car was parked outside now, with Kling leaning against the fender, his head erect, sweltering even in his summer blues. Tufts of blond hair stuck out of his lightweight hat. He was hot. He was hot as hell.

Inside, Carella was hot, too. "Where is he?" he asked Danny.

Danny rolled the ball of his thumb against the ball of his forefinger. "I haven't had a square meal in days," he said.

Carella took a ten spot from his wallet and fed it to Danny.

"He's at Mama Luz's," Danny said. "He's with a broad they call La Flamenca. She ain't so hot."

"What's he doing there?"

"He copped from a pusher a couple of hours back. Three decks of H. He stumbled over to Mama Luz with amorous intentions, but the H won the battle. Mama Luz tells me he's been dozing for the past sixty."

"And La Flamenca?"

"She's with him, probably cleaned out his wallet by this time. She's a big redheaded job with two gold teeth in the front of her mouth, damn near blind you with them teeth of hers. She's got mean hips, a big job, real big. Don't get rough with her, less she swallow you up in one gobble."

"Is he heeled?" Carella asked.

"Mama Luz don't know. She don't think so."

"Doesn't the redhead know?"

"I didn't ask the redhead," Danny said. "I don't deal with the hired help."

"Then how come you know about her hips?" Carella asked.

"Your ten spot don't buy my sex life," Danny said, smiling.

"Okay," Carella said, "thanks."

He left Danny at the table and went over to where Kling was leaning on the fender.

"Hot," Kling said.

"You want a beer, go ahead," Carella told him.

"No, I just want to go home."

"Everybody wants to go home," Carella said. "Home is where you pack your rod."

"I never understand detectives," Kling said.

"Come on, we have a visit to make," Carella said.

"Where?"

"Up the street. Mama Luz. Just point the car; it knows the way."

Kling took off his hat and ran one hand through his blond hair. "Phew," he said, and then he put on his hat and climbed in behind the wheel. "Who are we looking for?"

"Man named Dizzy Ordiz."

"Never heard of him."

"He never heard of you, either," Carella said.

"Yeah," Kling said dryly, "well, I'd appreciate it if you introduced us."

"I will," Carella said, and he smiled as Kling set the car in motion.

Mama Luz was standing in the doorway when they pulled up. The kids on the sidewalk wore big grins, expecting a raid. Mama Luz smiled and said, "Hello, Detective Carella. Hot, no?"

"Hot," Carella agreed, wondering why in hell everybody and his brother commented about the weather. It was certainly obvious to anyone but a half-wit that this was a very hot day, that this was a suffocatingly hot day, that this was probably hotter than a day in Manila, or even if you thought Calcutta hotter, this was still a lotta hotter heat than that.

Mama Luz was wearing a silk kimono. Mama Luz was a big fat woman with a mass of black hair pulled into a bun at the back of her head. Mama Luz used to be a well-known prostitute, allegedly one of the best in the city, but now she was a madam and never indulged, except for friends. She was scrupulously clean, and always smelled of lilacs. Her complexion was as white as any complexion can be, more white because it rarely saw the sun. Her features were patrician, her smile was angelic. If you didn't know she ran one of the wildest brothels on the Street, you might have thought she was somebody's mother.

She wasn't.

"You come on a social call?" she asked Carella, winking.

"If I can't have you, Mama Luz," Carella said, "I don't want anybody."

Kling blinked, and then wiped the sweatband of his hat.

"For you, *toro*," Mama Luz said, winking again, "Mama Luz does anything. For you, Mama Luz is a young girl again."

"You've always been a young girl," Carella said, and he slapped her on the backside, and then said, "Where's Ordiz?"

"With *la roja*," Mama Luz said. "She has picked his eyes out by now." She shrugged. "These new girls, all they are interested in is money. In the old days . . ." Mama Luz cocked her head wistfully. "In the old days, *toro*, there was sometimes love, do you know? What has happened to love nowadays, eh?"

"It's all locked up in that fat heart of yours," Carella said. "Does Ordiz have a gun?"

"Do I shake down my guests?" Mama Luz said. "I don't think he has a gun, Stevie. You will not shoot up the works, will you? This has been a quiet day."

"No, I will not shoot up the works," Carella said. "Show me where he is."

Mama Luz nodded. As Kling passed her, she looked down at his fly, and then laughed uproariously when he blushed. She followed the two cops in, and then passed them and said, "This way. Upstairs."

The stairs shook beneath her. She turned her head over her shoulder, winked at Carella, and said, "I trust you behind me, Stevie."

"Gracias," Carella said.

"Don't look up my dress."

"It's a temptation, I'll admit," Carella said, and behind him he heard Kling choke back a cross between a sob and a gasp.

Mama Luz stopped on the first landing. "The door at the end of the hall. No blood, Stevie, please. With this one, you do not need blood. He is half-dead already."

"Okay," Carella said. "Get downstairs, Mama Luz."

"And later, when the work is done," Mama Luz said suggestively, and she bumped one fleshy hip against Carella, almost knocking him off his feet. She went past Kling, laughing, her laughter trailing up the stairwell.

Carella sighed and looked at Kling. "What're you gonna do, kid," he said, "I'm in love."

"I never understand detectives," Kling said.

They went down the hallway. Kling drew his service revolver when he saw Carella's was already in his hand.

"She said no shooting," he reminded Carella.

"So far, she only runs a whore house," Carella said. "Not the Police Department."

"Sure," Kling said.

Carella rapped on the door with the butt of his .38.

"Quién es?" a girl's voice asked.

"Police," Carella said. "Open up."

"Momento," the voice said.

"She's getting dressed," Kling advised Carella.

In a few moments, the door opened. The girl

standing there was a big redhead. She was not smiling, so Carella did not have the opportunity to examine the gold teeth in the front of her mouth.

"What you want?" she asked.

"Clear out," Carella said. "We want to talk to the
man in there."

"Sure," she said. She threw Carella a look in-
tended to convey an attitude of virginity offended,
and then she swiveled past him and slithered down
the hallway. Kling watched her. When he turned
back to the door, Carella was already in the room.

There was a bed in the room, and a night table,
and a metal washbasin. The shade was drawn. The
room smelled badly. A man lay on the bed in his
trousers. His shoes and socks were off. His chest was
bare. His eyes were closed, and his mouth was open.
A fly buzzed around his nose.

"Open the window," Carella said to Kling. "Jesus,
this place stinks."

The man on the bed stirred. He lifted his head
and looked at Carella.

"Who are you?" he said.

"Your name Ordiz?" Carella asked.

"Yeah. You a cop?"

"Yes."

"What did I do wrong now?"

Kling opened the window. From the streets below
came the sound of children's voices.

"Where were you Sunday night?"

"What time?"

"Close to midnight."

"I don't remember."

"You better, Ordiz. You better start remembering damn fast. You shoot up just now?"

"I don't know what you mean."

"You're an H-man, Ordiz, and we know it, and we know you copped three decks a little while back. Are you stoned now, or can you read me?"

"I hear you," Ordiz said.

He passed a hand over his eyes. He owned a thin face with a hatchet nose and thick, rubbery lips. He needed a shave badly.

"Okay, talk."

"Friday night, you said?"

"I said Sunday."

"Sunday. Oh yeah. I was at a poker game."

"Where?"

"South 4th. What's the matter, you don't believe me?"

"You got witnesses?"

"Five guys in the game. You can check with any one of them."

"Give me their names."

"Sure. Louie DeScala, and his brother, John. Kid named Pete Diaz. Another kid they call Pepe. I don't know his last name."

"That's four," Carella said.

"I was the fifth."

"Where do these guys live?"

Ordiz reeled off a string of addresses.

"Okay, what about Monday night?"

"I was home."

"Anybody with you?"

"My landlady."

"What?"

"My landlady was with me. What's the matter, don't you hear good?"

"Shut up, Dizzy. What's her name?"

"Olga Pazio."

"Address?"

Ordiz gave it to him. "What am I supposed to done?" he asked.

"Nothing. You got a gun?"

"No. Listen, I been clean since I got out."

"What about those three decks?"

"I don't know where you got that garbage. Somebody's fooling you, cop."

"Sure. Get dressed, Dizzy."

"What for? I paid for the use of this pad."

"Okay, you used it already. Get dressed."

"Hey, listen, what for? I tell you I've been clean since I got out. What the hell, cop?"

"I want you at the precinct while I check these names. You mind?"

"They'll tell you I was with them, don't worry. And that junk about the three decks, Jesus, I don't know where you got that from. Hell, I ain't been near the stuff for years now."

"That's plain to see," Carella said. "Those scabs on your arm are from beri-beri or something, I guess."

"Huh?" Ordiz asked.

"Get dressed."

Carella checked with the men Ordiz had named. Each of them was willing to swear that he'd been at the poker game from ten-thirty on the night of July

23rd, to four A.M. on the morning of July 24th. Ordiz' landlady reluctantly admitted she had spent the night of the 24th and the morning of the 25th in Ordiz' room. Ordiz had solid alibis for the times someone had spent killing Reardon and Foster.

When Bush came back with his report on Flannagan, the boys were right back where they'd started.

"He's got an alibi as long as the Texas panhandle," Bush said.

Carella sighed, and then took Kling down for a beer before heading over to see Teddy.

Bush cursed the heat, and then went home to his wife.

10

From where Savage sat at the end of the bar, he could plainly see the scripted lettering on the back of the boy's brightly colored jacket. The boy had caught his eye the moment Savage entered the bar. He'd been sitting in a booth with a dark-haired girl, and they'd both been drinking beer. Savage had seen the purple and gold jacket and then sat at the bar and ordered a gin and tonic. From time to time, he'd glanced over at the couple. The boy was thin and pale, a shock of black hair crowning his head. The collar of the jacket was turned up, and Savage could not see the lettering across the back at first because the boy sat with his back tight against the padded cushioning of the booth.

The girl finished her beer and left, but the boy did not vacate the booth. He turned slightly, and that was when Savage saw the lettering, and that was when the insistent idea at the back of his mind began to take full shape and form.

The lettering on the jacket read: The Grovers.

The name had undoubtedly been taken from the

name of the park that hemmed in the 87th Precinct, but it was a name that rang a bell in Savage's head, and it didn't take long for that bell to begin echoing and re-echoing. The Grovers had been responsible for a good many of the street rumbles in the area, including an almost titanic struggle in one section of the park, a struggle featuring knives, broken bottles, guns, and sawed-off stickball bats. The Grovers had made their peace with the cops, or so the story went, but the persistent idea that one of the gangs was responsible for the deaths of Reardon and Foster would not leave Savage's mind.

And here was a Grover.

Here was a boy to talk to.

Savage finished his gin and tonic, left his stool, and walked over to where the boy was sitting alone in the booth.

"Hi," he said.

The boy did not move his head. He raised only his eyes. He said nothing.

"Mind if I sit down?" Savage asked.

"Beat it, mister," the boy said.

Savage reached into his jacket pocket. The boy watched him silently. He took out a package of cigarettes, offered one to the boy and, facing the silent refusal, hung one on his own lip.

"My name's Savage," he said.

"Who cares?" the boy answered.

"I'd like to talk to you."

"Yeah? What about?"

"The Grovers."

"Mister, you don't live around here, do you?"

"No."

"Then, Dad, go home."

"I told you. I want to talk."

"I don't. I'm waitin' for a deb. Take off while you still got legs."

"I'm not scared of you, kid, so knock off the rough talk."

The boy appraised Savage coolly.

"What's your name?" Savage asked.

"Guess, Blondie."

"You want a beer?"

"You buying?"

"Sure," Savage said.

"Then make it a rum-coke."

Savage turned toward the bar. "Rum-coke," he called, "and another gin and tonic."

"You drink gin, huh?" the boy said.

"Yes. What's your name, son?"

"Rafael," the boy said, still studying Savage closely. "The guys call me Rip."

"Rip. That's a good name."

"Good as any. What's the matter, you don't like it?"

"I like it," Savage said.

"You a nab?"

"A what?"

"A cop."

"No."

"What then?"

"I'm a reporter."

"Yeah?"

"Yes."

"So whatya want from me?"

"I only want to talk."

"What about?"

"Your gang."

"What gang?" Rip said. "I don't belong to no gang."

The waiter brought the drinks. Rip tasted his and said, "That bartender's a crook. He cuts the juice here. This tastes like cream soda."

"Here's luck," Savage said.

"You're gonna need it," Rip replied.

"About The Grovers . . ."

"The Grovers are a club."

"Not a gang?"

"Whatta we need a gang for? We're a club, that's all."

"Who's president?" Savage asked.

"That's for me to know and you to find out," Rip answered.

"What's the matter? You ashamed of the club?"

"Hell, no."

"Don't you want to see it publicized in a newspaper? There isn't another club in the neighborhood that ever got a newspaper's full treatment."

"We don't need no treatment. We got a big rep as it is. Ain't nobody in this city who ain't heard of The Grovers. Who you tryin' to snow, mister?"

"Nobody. I just thought you'd like some public relations work."

"What the hell's that?"

"A favorable press."

"You mean . . ." Rip furrowed his brow. "What do you mean?"

"An article telling about your club."

"We don't need no articles. You better cut out, Dad."

"Rip, I'm trying to be your friend."

"I got plenty friends in The Grovers."

"How many?"

"There must be at least . . ." Rip stopped short. "You're a wise bastard, ain't you?"

"You don't have to tell me anything you don't want to, Rip. Why do the boys call you 'Rip'?"

"We all got nicknames. That's mine."

"But why?"

"Because I can handle a blade good."

"Did you ever have to?"

"Handle one? You kidding? In this neighborhood, you don't carry a knife or a piece, you're dead. Dead, man."

"What's a piece, Rip?"

"A gun." Rip opened his eyes wide. "You don't know what a piece is? Man, you ain't been."

"Do The Grovers have many pieces?"

"Enough."

"What kind?"

"All kinds. What do you want? We got it."

".45's?"

"Why do you ask?"

"Nice gun, a .45."

"Yeah, it's big," Rip said.

"Do you ever use these pieces?"

"You got to use them. Man, you think these did-dlebops are for fun? You got to use whatever you can get your hands on. Otherwise, you wind up with a tag on your toe." Rip drank a little more of the rum. "This neighborhood ain't a cream puff, Dad. You got to watch yourself all the time. That's why it helps to belong to The Grovers. They see this jacket comin' down the street, they got respect. They know if they mess with me, they got *all* The Grovers to mess with."

"The police, you mean?"

"Naw, who wants Law trouble? We steer away from them. Unless they bother us."

"Any cops bother you lately?"

"We got a thing on with the cops. They don't bother us, we don't bother them. Man, there ain't been a rumble in months. Things are very quiet."

"You like it that way?"

"Sure, why not? Who wants his skull busted? The Grovers want peace. We never punk out, but we never go lookin' for trouble, either. Only time we get involved is when we're challenged, or when a stud from another club tries to make it with one of our debs. We don't go for that kind of crap."

"So you've had no trouble with the police lately?"

"Few little skirmishes. Nothing to speak of."

"What kind of skirmishes?"

"Agh, one of the guys was on mootah. So he got a little high, you know. So he busted a store window, for kicks, you know? So one of the cops put the arm on him. He got a suspended sentence."

"*Who* put the arm on him?"

"Why you want to know?"

"I'm just curious."

"One of the bulls, I don't remember who."

"A detective?"

"I said a bull, didn't I?"

"How'd the rest of The Grovers feel about this?"

"How do you mean?"

"About this detective pulling in one of your boys?"

"Agh, the kid was a Junior, didn't know his ass from his elbow. Nobody shoulda given him a reefer to begin with. You don't handle a reefer right... well, you know, the guy was just a kid."

"And you felt no resentment for the cop who'd pulled him in?"

"Huh?"

"You had nothing against the cop who pulled him in?"

Rip's eyes grew suddenly wary. "What're you drivin' at, mister?"

"Nothing, really."

"What'd you say your name was?"

"Savage."

"Why you askin' about how we feel about cops?"

"No reason."

"Then why you askin'?"

"I was just curious."

"Yeah," Rip said flatly. "Well, I got to go now. I guess that deb ain't comin' back."

"Listen, stick around a while," Savage said. "I'd like to talk some more."

"Yeah?"

"Yes, I would."

"That's tough, pal," Rip said. "I wouldn't." He got out of the booth. "Thanks for the drink. I see you around."

"Sure," Savage said.

He watched the boy's shuffling walk as he moved out of the bar. The door closed behind him, and he was gone.

Savage studied his drink. There *had* been trouble between The Grovers and a cop—a detective, in fact. So his theory was not quite as far-fetched as the good lieutenant tried to make it.

He sipped at his drink, thinking, and when he'd finished it, he ordered another. He walked out of the bar about ten minutes later, passing two neatly dressed men on his way out.

The two men were Steve Carella and a patrolman in street clothes—a patrolman named Bert Kling.

11

Bush was limp when he reached the apartment.

He hated difficult cases, but only because he felt curiously inadequate to cope with them. He had not been joking when he told Carella he felt detectives weren't particularly brilliant men. He thoroughly believed this, and whenever a difficult case popped up, his faith in his own theory was reaffirmed.

Legwork and stubbornness, that was all it amounted to.

So far, the legwork they'd done had brought them no closer to the killer than they originally were. The stubbornness? Well, that was another thing again. They would keep at it, of course. Until the break came. When would the break come? Today? Tomorrow? Never?

The hell with the case, he thought. I'm home. A man is entitled to the luxury of leaving his goddamn job at the office. A man is entitled to a few peaceful hours with his wife.

He pushed his key into the lock, twisted it, and then threw the door open.

"Hank?" Alice called.

"Yes." Her voice sounded cool. Alice always sounded cool. Alice was a remarkable woman.

"Do you want a drink?"

"Yes. Where are you?"

"In the bedroom. Come on in, there's a nice breeze here."

"A breeze? You're kidding."

"No, seriously."

He took off his jacket and threw it over the back of a chair. He was pulling off his shirt as he went into the bedroom. Bush never wore undershirts. He did not believe in the theory of sweat absorption. An undershirt, he held, was simply an additional piece of wearing apparel, and in this weather the idea was to get as close to the nude as possible. He ripped off his shirt with almost savage intensity. He had a broad chest matted with curling red hair that matched the thatch on his head. The knife scar ran its crooked path down his right arm.

Alice lay in a chaise near the open window. She wore a white blouse and a straight black skirt. She was barefoot, and her legs were propped up on the windowsill, and the black skirt rustled mildly with the faint breeze that came through the window. She had drawn her blond hair back into a ponytail. He went to her, and she lifted her face for his kiss, and he noticed the thin film of perspiration on her upper lip.

"Where's that drink?" he asked.

"I'll mix it," she said. She swung her feet off the windowsill, and the skirt pulled back for an instant, her thigh winking at him. He watched her silently, wondering what it was about this woman that was so exciting, wondering if all married men felt this way about their wives even after ten years of marriage.

"Get that gleam out of your eyes," she said, reading his face.

"Why?"

"It's too damn hot."

"I know a fellow who claims the best way . . ."

"I know about that fellow."

"Is in a locked room on the hottest day of the year with the windows closed under four blankets."

"Gin and tonic?"

"Good."

"I heard that vodka and tonic is better."

"We'll have to get some."

"Busy day at the mine?"

"Yes. You?"

"Sat around and worried about you," Alice said.

"I see all those grey hairs sprouting."

"He belittles my concern," Alice said to the air. "Did you find that killer yet?"

"No."

"Do you want a lime in this?"

"If you like."

"Means going into the kitchen. Be a doll and drink it this way."

"I'm a doll," Bush said.

She handed him the drink. Bush sat on the edge of the bed. He sipped at the drink, and then leaned forward, the glass dangling at the ends of his long muscular arms.

"Tired?"

"Pooped."

"You don't look very tired."

"I'm so pooped, I'm peeped."

"You always say that," Alice said. "I wish you wouldn't always say that. There are things you always say."

"Like what?"

"Well, like that, for one."

"Name another."

"When we're driving in the car and there are fixed traffic signals. Whenever you begin hitting the lights right, you say 'We're in with the boys.' "

"So what's wrong with that?"

"Nothing, the first hundred times."

"Oh, hell."

"Well, it's true."

"All right, all right. I'm not peeped. I'm not even pooped."

"I'm hot," Alice said.

"So am I."

She began unbuttoning her blouse, and even before he looked up, she said, "Don't get ideas."

She took off the blouse and draped it over the back of the chaise. She owned large breasts, and they were crowded into a filmy white brassiere. The front slope of the cups was covered with a sheer nylon inset, and he could see the insistent pucker of her nipples. It reminded him of pictures he had seen in *National Geographic* at the dentist's office, the time he'd had that periodontal work done. The girls on Bali. Nobody had breasts like the girls on Bali. Except maybe Alice.

"What'd you do all day?" he asked.

"Nothing much."

"Were you in?"

"Most of the time."

"So what'd you do?"

"Sat around, mostly."

"Mmmm." He could not take his eyes from the brassiere. "Did you miss me?"

"I always miss you," she said flatly.

"I missed you."

"Drink your drink."

"No, really."

"Well, good," she said, and she smiled fleetingly. He studied the smile. It was gone almost instantly, and he had the peculiar feeling that it had been nothing more than a duty smile.

"Why don't you get some sleep?" she asked.

"Not yet," he said, watching her.

"Hank, if you think . . ."

"What?"

"Nothing."

"I've got to go in again later," he said.

"They're really pushing on this one, aren't they?"

"Lots of pressure," he said. "I think the Old Man is scared he's next."

"I'll bet it's all over," Alice said. "I don't think there'll be another killing."

"You can never tell," Bush said.

"Do you want something to eat before you turn in?" she asked.

"I'm not turning in yet."

Alice sighed. "You can't escape this damn heat," she said. "No matter what you do, it's always with you." Her hand went to the button at the side of her skirt. She undid it, and then pulled down the zipper. The skirt slid to her feet, and she stepped out of it. She was wearing white nylon panties frilled with a gossamer web of puffed nylon at each leg. She walked to the window, and he watched her. Her legs were long and clean.

"Come here," he said.

"No. I don't want to, Hank."

"All right," he said.

"Do you think it'll cool off tonight?"

"I doubt it." He watched her closely. He had the distinct impression that she was undressing for him, and yet she'd said . . . He tweaked his nose, puzzled.

She turned from the window. Her skin was very white against the white of her underwear. Her breasts bulged over the edges of the inadequate bra. "You need a haircut," she said.

"I'll try to get one tomorrow. We haven't had a minute."

"Oh, goddamn this heat, anyway," she said, and she reached behind her to unclasp the bra. He watched her breasts spill free, watched as she tossed the bra across the room. She walked to mix herself another drink, and he could not take his eyes from her. *What's she trying to do?* he wondered. *What the hell is she trying to do to me?*

He rose swiftly, walking to where she stood. He put his arms around her, and his hands cupped her breasts.

"Don't," she said.

"Baby . . ."

"Don't." Her voice was firm, a cold edge to it.

"Why not?"

"Because I say so."

"Well, then why the hell are you parading around like . . ."

"Take your hands off me, Hank. Let me go."

"Aw, baby . . ."

She broke away from him. "Get some sleep," she said. "You're tired." There was something strange in her eyes, an almost malicious gleam.

"Can't . . ."

"No."

"For Christ's sake, Alice . . ."

"No!"

"All right."

She smiled quickly. "All right," she repeated.

"Well . . ." Bush paused. "I'd . . . I'd better get to bed."

"Yes. You'd better."

"What I can't understand is why . . ."

"You won't even need a sheet in this weather," Alice interrupted.

"No, I guess not."

He went to the bed and took off his shoes and socks. He didn't want to undress because he didn't want to give her the satisfaction, now that he'd been denied, of knowing how she'd affected him. He took off his trousers and quickly got into the bed, pulling the sheet to his throat.

Alice watched him, smiling. "I'm reading *Anapurna,*" she said.

"So?"

"I just happened to think of it."

Bush rolled over onto his side.

"I'm still hot," Alice said. "I think I'll take a shower. And then maybe I'll catch an air-conditioned movie. You don't mind, do you?"

"No," Bush mumbled.

She walked to the side of the bed and stood there for a moment, looking down at him. "Yes, I think I'll take a shower." Her hands went to her hips. Slowly, she rolled the panties down over the flatness of her stomach, past the hard jut of her crotch, over the whiteness of her thighs. The panties dropped to the floor, and she stepped out of them and stood by the bed, looking down at Bush, smiling.

He did not move. He kept his eyes on the floor, but he could see her feet and her legs, but he did not move.

"Sleep tight, darling," she whispered, and then she went into the bathroom.

He heard the shower when it began running. He lay on the soggy sheet and listened to the steady machine-gunning of the water. Then, over the sound of the shower, came the sound of the telephone, splitting the silence of the room.

He sat up and reached for the instrument.

"Hello?"

"Bush?"

118   ED McBAIN

"Yes?"

"This is Havilland. You better get down here right away."

"What's the matter?" Bush asked.

"You know that young rookie Kling?"

"Yeah?"

"He was just shot in a bar on Culver."

12

The squad room of the 87th resembled nothing so much as the locker room of the Boys' Club when Bush arrived. There must have been at least two dozen teenagers crammed in behind the dividing rail and the desks beyond it. Add to this a dozen or so detectives who were firing questions, the answers to which were coming in two languages, and the bedlam was equivalent to the hush of a hydrogen bomb explosion.

The boys were all wearing brilliantly contrasting purple and gold jackets, and the words "The Grovers" decorated the back of each jacket. Bush looked for Carella in the crowded room, spotted him, and walked over toward him quickly. Havilland, a tough cop with a cherubic face, shouted at one of the boys, "Don't give me any guff, you little punk, or I'll break your goddamn arm."

"You try it, dick," the kid answered, and Havilland cuffed him across the mouth. The boy staggered back, slamming into Bush as he went by. Bush shrugged his shoulders, and the boy flew back into

Havilland's arms, as if he'd been brushed aside by a
rhinoceros.

Carella was talking to two boys when Bush ap-
proached him.

"Who fired the gun?" he asked.

The boys shrugged.

"We'll throw you all in jail as accessories," Carella
promised.

"What the hell happened?" Bush wanted to
know.

"I was having a beer with Kling. Nice, peaceful,
off-duty beer. I left him there, and ten minutes later,
when he's leaving the joint, he gets jumped by these
punks. One of them put a slug in him."

"How is he?"

"He's at the hospital. The slug was a .22, went
through his right shoulder. We figure a zip gun."

"You think this ties with the other kills?"

"I doubt it. The m.o.'s way off."

"Then why?"

"How the hell do I know? Looks like the whole
city figures it's open season on cops." Carella turned
back to the boys. "Were you with the gang when the
cop was jumped?"

The boys would not answer.

"Okay, fellas," Carella said, "play it smart. See what
that gets you. See how long The Grovers are gonna
last under a rap like this one."

"We din' shoot no cop," one of the boys said.

"No? What happened, he shoot himself?"

"You ting we crazy?" the other boy said. "Shoot a
bull?"

"This was a patrolman," Carella said, "not a detective."

"He wass wear a suit," the first boy said.

"Cops wear suits off-duty," Bush said. "Now how about it?"

"Nobody shoot a cop," the first boy said.

"No, except somebody did."

Lieutenant Byrnes came out of his office and shouted, "All right, knock it off! KNOCK IT OFF!"

The room fell immediately silent.

"Who's your talk man?" Byrnes asked.

"I am," a tall boy answered.

"What's your name?"

"Do-Do."

"What's your full name?"

"Salvador Jesus Santez."

"All right, come here, Salvador."

"The guys call me Do-Do."

"Okay, come here."

Santez walked over to where Byrnes was standing. He walked with a shuffle which was considered both hip and cool. The boys in the room visibly relaxed. This was their talk man, and Do-Do was a real gone stud. Do-Do would know how to handle this jive.

"What happened?" Byrnes asked.

"Little skirmish, that's all," Santez said.

"Why?"

"Jus' like that. We got the word passed down, so we joined the fray."

"What word?"

"You know, like a scout was out."

"No, I don't know. What the hell are you talking about?"

"Look, Dad . . ." Santez started.

"You call me 'Dad' again," Byrnes warned, "and I'll beat you black and blue."

"Well, gee, Da . . ." Santez stopped dead. "What you want to know?"

"I want to know why you jumped a cop."

"What cop? What're you talkin' about?"

"Look, Santez, don't play this too goddamn cute. You jumped one of our patrolmen as he came out of a bar. You beat him up, and one of your boys put a bullet in his shoulder. Now what the hell's the story?"

Santez considered Byrnes' question gravely.

"Well?"

"He's a cop?"

"What the hell did you think he was?"

"He was wearing a light blue summer suit!" Santez said, his eyes opening wide.

"What the hell's that got to do with it? Why'd you jump him? Why'd you shoot him?"

A mumbling was starting behind Santez. Byrnes heard the mumble and shouted, "Shut up! You've got your talk man, let *him* talk!"

Santez was still silent.

"What about it, Santez?"

"A mistake," Santez said.

"That's for damn sure."

"I mean, we didn't know he was a cop."

"Why'd you jump him?"

"A mistake, I tell you."

"Start from the beginning."

"Okay," Santez said. "We been giving you trouble lately?"

"No."

"Okay. We been minding our own business, right? You never hear from The Grovers, except when we protectin' our own, right? The last rumble you get is over there in The Silver Culvers' territory when they pick on one of our Juniors. Am I right?"

"Go ahead, Santez."

"Okay. Early today, there's a guy snooping around. He grabs one of our Seniors in a bar, and he starts pumpin' him."

"Which Senior?"

"I forget," Santez said.

"Who was the guy?"

"Said he was from a newspaper."

"What?"

"Yeah. Said his name was Savage, you know him?"

"I know him," Byrnes said tightly.

"Okay, so he starts askin' like how many pieces we got, and whether we got .45's, and whether we don't like the Law, things like that. This Senior, he's real hip. He tips right off this guy is trying to mix in The Grovers with the two bulls got knocked off around here. So he's on a newspaper, and we got a rep to protect. We don't want Law trouble. If this jerk goes back to his paper and starts printing lies about how we're mixed in, that ain't good for our rep."

"So what'd you do, Santez?" Byrnes asked wearily, thinking of Savage, and thinking of how he'd like to wring the reporter's neck.

"So this Senior comes back, and we planned to scare off the reporter before he goes printing any crap. We went back to the bar and waited for him. When he come out, we jumped him. Only he pulled a gun, so one of the boys plugged him in self-defense."

"Who?"

"Who knows?" Santez said. "One of the boys burned him."

"Thinking he was Savage."

"Sure. How the hell we supposed to know he's a cop instead? He had on a light blue suit, and he had blond hair, like this reporter creep. So we burned him. It was a mistake."

"You keep saying that, Santez, but I don't think you know just how big a mistake it was. Who fired that shot?"

Santez shrugged.

"Who was the Senior Savage talked to?"

Santez shrugged.

"Is he here?"

Santez had stopped talking, it seemed.

"You know we've got a list of every damn member in your gang, don't you, Santez?"

"Sure."

"Okay. Havilland, get the list. I want a roll call. Whoever's not here, pick him up."

"Hey, wait a minute," Santez said. "I told you it was all a mistake. You going to get somebody in trouble just 'cause we mistake a cop?"

"Listen to me, Santez, and listen hard. Your gang hasn't been in any trouble recently, and that's fine with us. Call it a truce, call it whatever you want to. But don't ever think, and I mean *ever*, Santez, that you or your boys can shoot anybody in this goddamn precinct and get away with it. You're a bunch of hoods as far as I'm concerned, Santez. You're a bunch of hoods with fancy jackets, and a seventeen-year-old hood is no less dangerous than a fifty-year-old hood. The only reason we haven't been bearing down on you is because you've been behaving yourself. All right, today you stopped behaving yourself. You shot a man in my precinct territory—and that means you're in trouble. That means you're in big trouble."

Santez blinked.

"Put them all downstairs and call the roll there," Byrnes said. "Then get whoever we missed."

"All right, let's go," Havilland said. He began herding the boys out of the room.

Miscolo, one of the patrolmen from Clerical, pushed his way through the crowd and walked over to the lieutenant.

"Lieutenant, fella outside wants to see you," he said.

"Who?"

"Guy named Savage. Claims he's a reporter. Wants to know what the rumble was about this aft—"

"Kick him down the steps," Byrnes said, and he went back into his office.

13

Homicide, if it doesn't happen too close to home, is a fairly interesting thing.

You can really get involved in the investigation of a homicide case because it is the rare occurrence in the everyday life of a precinct. It is the most exotic crime because it deals with the theft of something universal—a man's life.

Unfortunately, there are other less interesting and more mundane matters to deal with in a precinct, too. And in a precinct like the 87th, these mundane matters can consume a lot of time. There are the rapes, and the muggings, and the rollings, and the knifings, and the various types of disorderly conducts, and the breakings and entries, and the burglaries, and the car thefts, and the street rumbles, and the cats caught in sewers, and oh, like that. Many of these choice items of crime are promptly turned over to special squads within the department, but the initial squeal nonetheless goes to the precinct in which the crime is being committed, and these squeals can keep a man hopping.

It's not so easy to hop when the temperature is high.

For cops, shocking as the notion may sound at first, are human beings. They sweat like you and me, and they don't like to work when it's hot. Some of them don't like to work even when it's cool. None of them like to draw Lineup, especially when it's hot.

Steve Carella and Hank Bush drew Lineup on Thursday, July 27th.

They were especially displeased about it because Lineup is held only from Mondays to Thursdays, and if they had missed it this Thursday, chances were they would not pull the duty until the following week and perhaps—just perhaps—the heat would have broken by then.

The morning started the way most mornings were starting that week. There was a deceptive coolness at first, a coolness which—despite the prognostications of television's various weather men and weather women—seemed to promise a delightful day ahead. The delusions and flights of fancy fled almost instantly. It was apparent within a half-hour of being awake that this was going to be another scorcher, that you would meet people who asked, "Hot enough for you?" or who blandly and informatively remarked, "It's not the heat; it's the humidity."

Whatever it was, it was hot.

It was hot where Carella lived in the suburb of Riverhead, and it was hot in the heart of the city—on High Street, where Headquarters and the lineup awaited.

Since Bush lived in another suburb—Calm's

Point, west and a little south of Riverhead—they chose to meet at Headquarters at 8:45, fifteen minutes before the lineup began. Carella was there on the dot.

At 8:50, Bush strolled up. That is to say, he more or less crawled onto the pavement and slouched over to where Carella was standing and puffing on a cigarette.

"Now I know what Hell is like," he said.

"Wait until the sun really starts shining," Carella said.

"You cheerful guys are always good for an early morning laugh," Bush answered. "Let me have a cigarette, will you?"

Carella glanced at his watch. "Time we were up there."

"Let it wait. We've got a few minutes yet." He took the cigarette Carella offered, lighted it, and blew out a stream of smoke. "Any new corpses today?"

"None yet."

"Pity. I'm getting so I miss my morning coffee and corpse."

"The city," Carella said.

"What?"

"Look at it. What a goddamn monster."

"A hairy bastard," Bush agreed.

"But I love her."

"Yeah," Bush said noncommittally.

"It's too hot to work today. This is a day for the beach."

"The beaches'll be jammed. You're lucky you've got a nice lineup to attend."

"Sure, I know. Who wants a cool, sandy beach with the breakers rolling in and . . ."

"You Chinese?"

"Huh?"

"You know your torture pretty good."

"Let's go upstairs."

They flipped their cigarettes away and entered the Headquarters building. The building had once boasted clean red brick and architecture which was modern. The brick was now covered with the soot of five decades, and the architecture was as modern as a chastity belt.

They walked into the first-floor marbled entryway, past the dick squad room, past the lab, past the various records rooms. Down a shaded hallway, a frosted glass door announced "Commissioner of Police."

"I'll bet *he's* at the beach," Carella said.

"He's in there hiding behind his desk," Bush said. "He's afraid the 87th's maniac is going to get him next."

"Maybe he's not at the beach," Carella amended. "I understand this building has a swimming pool in the basement."

"Two of them," Bush said. He rang for the elevator. They waited in hot, suffering silence for several moments. The elevator doors slid open. The patrolman inside was sweating.

"Step into the iron coffin," he said.

Carella grinned. Bush winced. Together they got into the car.

"Lineup?" the patrolman asked.

"No, the swimming pool," Bush cracked.

"Jokes I can't take in this heat," the patrolman said.

"Then don't supply straight lines," Bush said.

"Abbott and Costello I've got with me," the patrolman said, and then he lapsed into silence. The elevator crawled up the intestinal tract of the building. It creaked. It whined. Its walls were moist with the beaded exhalations of its occupants.

"Nine," the patrolman said.

The doors slid open. Carella and Bush stepped into a sunlit corridor. Simultaneously, they reached for the leather cases to which their shields were pinned. Again simultaneously, they pinned the tin to their collars and then walked toward the desk behind which another patrolman was seated.

The patrolman eyed the tin, nodded, and they passed the desk and walked into a large room which served many purposes at Headquarters. The room was built with the physical proportions of a gymnasium, and did indeed have two basketball hoops, one at each end of the room. The windows were wide and tall, covered with steel mesh. The room was used for indoor sport, lectures, swearing in of rookies, occasional meetings of the Police Benevolent Association or the Police Honor Legion and, of course, the lineups.

For the purpose of these Monday-to-Thursday parades of felony offenders, a permanent stage had been set up at the far end of the room, beneath the balcony there, and beyond the basketball hoop. The stage was brilliantly lighted. Behind the stage was a white wall, and upon the wall in black numerals was the graduated height scale against which the prisoners stood.

In front of the stage, and stretching back toward the entrance doorways for about ten rows, was an array of folding chairs, most of which were occupied by detectives from all over the city when Bush and Carella entered. The blinds at the windows had already been drawn, and a look at the raised dais and speaking stand behind the chairs showed that the Chief of Detectives was already in position and the strawberry festival would start in a few moments. To the left of the stage, the felony offenders huddled in a group, lightly guarded by several patrolmen and several detectives, the men who had made the arrests. Every felony offender who'd been picked up in the city the day before would be paraded across the stage this morning.

The purpose of the lineup, you see—despite popular misconception about the identification of suspects by victims, a practice which was more helpful in theory than in actual usage—was simply to acquaint as many detectives as possible with the men who were doing evil in their city. The ideal setup would have been to have each detective in each precinct at each scheduled lineup, but other pressing matters made this impossible. So two men were chosen each day from each precinct, on the theory that if you can't acquaint all of the people all of the time, you can at least acquaint some of them some of the time.

"All right," the Chief of Detectives said into his microphone, "let's start."

Carella and Bush took seats in the fifth row as the first two offenders walked onto the stage. It was the practice to show the offenders as they'd been picked up, in pairs, in a trio, a quartet, whatever. This simply for the purpose of establishing an m.o. If a crook works in a pair once, he will generally work in a pair again.

The police stenographer poised his pen above his pad. The Chief of Detectives intoned, "Diamondback, One," calling off the area of the city in which the arrest had been made, and the number of the case from that area that day. "Diamondback, One. Anselmo, Joseph, 17, and Di Palermo, Frederick, 16. Forced the door of an apartment on Cambridge and Gribble. Occupant screamed for help, bringing patrolman to scene. No statement. How about it, Joe?"

Joseph Anselmo was a tall, thin boy with dark black hair and dark brown eyes. The eyes seemed darker than they were because they were set against a pale, white face. The whiteness was attributable to one emotion, and one emotion alone. Joseph Anselmo was scared.

"How about it, Joe?" the Chief of Detectives asked again.

"What do you want to know?" Anselmo said.

"Did you force the door to that apartment?"

"Yes."

"Why?"

"I don't know."

"Well, you forced a door, you must have had a reason for doing it. Did you know somebody was in the apartment?"

"No."

"Did you force it alone?"

Anselmo did not answer.

"How about it, Freddie. Were you with Joe when you broke that lock?"

Frederick Di Palermo was blond and blue-eyed. He was shorter than Anselmo, and he looked cleaner. He shared two things in common with his friend. First, he had been picked up on a felony offense. Second, he was scared.

"I was with him," Di Palermo said.

"How'd you force the door?"

"We hit the lock."

"What with?"

"A hammer."

"Weren't you afraid it would make noise?"

"We only give it a quick rap," Di Palermo said. "We didn't know somebody was home."

"What'd you expect to get in that apartment?" the Chief of Detectives asked.

"I don't know," Di Palermo said.

"Now, look," the Chief of Detectives said patiently, "you both broke into an apartment. Now we know that, and you just admitted it, so you must have had a reason for going in there. What do you say?"

"The girls told us," Anselmo said.

"What girls?"

"Oh, some chicks," Di Palermo answered.

"What'd they tell you?"

"To bust the door."

"Why?"

"Like that," Anselmo said.

"Like what?"

"Like for kicks."

"Only for kicks?"

"I don't know why we busted the door," Anselmo said, and he glanced quickly at Di Palermo.

"To take something out of the apartment?" the Chief asked.

"Maybe a . . ." Di Palermo shrugged.

"Maybe what?"

"A couple of bucks. You know, like that."

"You were planning a burglary then, is that right?"

"Yeah, I guess."

"What'd you do when you discovered the apartment was occupied?"

"The lady screamed," Anselmo said.

"So we run," Di Palermo said.

"Next case," the Chief of Detectives said.

The boys shuffled off the stage to where their arresting officer was waiting for them. Actually, they had said a hell of a lot more than they should have. They'd have been within their rights if they'd insisted on not saying a word at the lineup. Not knowing this, not even knowing that their position was fortified because they'd made no statement when they'd been collared, they had answered the Chief of Detectives with remarkable naïveté. A good lawyer, with a simple charge of unlawfully entering under circumstances or in a manner not amounting to a burglary, would have had his clients plead guilty to a misdemeanor. The Chief of Detectives, however, had asked the boys if they were planning to commit a burglary, and the boys had answered in the affirmative. And the Penal Law, Section 402, defines Burglary in first degree thusly:

> A person, who, with intent to commit some crime therein, breaks and enters, in the night time, the dwelling-house of another, in which there is at the time a human being:
> 1. Being armed with a dangerous weapon; or
> 2. Arming himself therein with such a weapon; or
> 3. Being assisted by a confederate actually present; or . . .

Well, no matter. The boys had very carelessly tied the knot of a felony about their youthful necks, perhaps not realizing that burglary in the first degree is punishable by imprisonment in a state prison for an indeterminate term the minimum of which shall not be less than ten years and the maximum of which shall not be more than thirty years.

Apparently, "the girls" had told them wrong.

"Diamondback, Two," the Chief of Detectives said. "Pritchett, Virginia, 34. Struck her quote husband unquote about the neck and head with a hatchet at three A.M. in the morning. No statement."

Virginia Pritchett had walked onto the stage while the Chief of Detectives was talking. She was a small woman, barely clearing the five-foot-one-inch marker. She was thin, narrow-boned, with red hair of the fine, spider-webby type. She wore no lipstick. She wore no smile. Her eyes were dead.

"Virginia?" the Chief of Detectives said.

She raised her head. She kept her hands close to her waist, one fist folded over the other. Her eyes did not come to life. They were grey, and she stared into the glaring lights unblinkingly.

"Virginia?"

"Yes, sir?" Her voice was very soft, barely audible. Carella leaned forward to catch what she was saying.

"Have you ever been in trouble before, Virginia?" the Chief of Detectives asked.

"No, sir."

"What happened, Virginia?"

The girl shrugged, as if she too could not comprehend what had happened. The shrug was a small one, a gesture that would have been similar to passing a hand over the eyes.

"What happened, Virginia?"

The girl raised herself up to her full height, partly to speak into the permanently fixed microphone which dangled several inches before her face on a solid steel pipe, partly because there were eyes on her and because she apparently realized her shoulders were slumped. The room was deathly still. There was not a breeze in the city. Beyond the glaring lights, the detectives sat.

"We argued," she said, sighing.

"Do you want to tell us about it?"

"We argued from the morning, from when we first got up. The heat. It's . . . it was very hot in the apartment. Right from the morning. You . . . you lose your temper quickly in the heat."

"Go on."

"He started with the orange juice. He said the orange juice wasn't cold enough. I told him I'd had it in the icebox all night, it wasn't my fault it wasn't cold. Diamondback isn't ritzy, sir. We don't have refrigerators in Diamondback, and with this heat, the ice melts very fast. Well, he started complaining about the orange juice."

"Were you married to this man?"

"No, sir."

"How long have you been living together?"

"Seven years, sir."

"Go on."

"He said he was going down for breakfast, and I said he shouldn't go down because it was silly to spend money when you didn't have to. He stayed, but he complained about the orange juice all the while he ate. It went on like that all day."

"About the orange juice, you mean?"

"No, other things. I don't remember what. He was watching the ball game on TV, and drinking beer, and he'd pick on little things all day long. He was sitting in his undershorts because of the heat. I had hardly anything on myself."

"Go on."

"We had supper late, just cold cuts. He was picking on me all that time. He didn't want to sleep in the bedroom that night, he wanted to sleep on the kitchen floor. I told him it was silly, even though the bedroom is very hot. He hit me."

"What do you mean, he hit you?"

"He hit me about the face. He closed one eye for me. I told him not to touch me again, or I would push him out the window. He laughed. He put a blanket on the kitchen floor, near the window, and he turned on the radio, and I went into the bedroom to sleep."

"Yes, go ahead, Virginia."

"I couldn't sleep because it was so hot. And he had the radio up loud. I went into the kitchen to tell him to please put the radio a little lower, and he said to go back to bed. I went into the bathroom, and I washed my face, and that was when I spied the hatchet."

"Where was the hatchet?"

"He keeps tools on a shelf in the bathroom, wrenches and a hammer, and the hatchet was with them. I thought I would go out and tell him to put the radio lower again, because it was very hot and the radio was very loud, and I wanted to try to get some sleep. But I didn't want him to hit me again, so I took the hatchet, to protect myself with, in case he tried to get rough again."

"Then what did you do?"

"I went out into the kitchen with the hatchet in my hands. He had got up off the floor and was sitting in a chair near the window, listening to the radio. His back was to me."

"Yes."

"I walked over to him, and he didn't turn around, and I didn't say anything to him."

"What did you do?"

"I struck him with the hatchet."

"Where?"

"On his head and on his neck."

"How many times?"

"I don't remember exactly. I just kept hitting him."

"Then what?"

"He fell off the chair, and I dropped the hatchet, and I went next door to Mr. Alanos, he's our neighbor, and I told him I had hit my husband with a hatchet, and he didn't believe me. He came into the apartment, and then he called the police, and an officer came."

"Your husband was taken to the hospital, did you know that?"

"Yes."

"Do you know the disposition of his case?"

Her voice was very low. "I heard he died," she said. She lowered her head and did not look out past the lights again. Her fists were still folded at her waist. Her eyes were still dead.

"Next case," the Chief of Detectives said.

"She *murdered* him," Bush whispered, his voice curiously loaded with awe. Carella nodded.

"Majesta, One," the Chief of Detectives said. "Bronckin, David, 27. Had a lamp outage report at 10:24 P.M. last night, corner of Weaver and 69th North. Electric company notified at once, and then another lamp outage two blocks south reported, and then gunfire reported. Patrolman picked up Bronckin on Dicsen and 69th North. Bronckin was intoxicated, was going down the street shooting out lamppost fixtures. What about it, Dave?"

"I'm only Dave to my friends," Bronckin said.

"What about it?"

"What do you want from me? I got high, I shot out a few lights. I'll pay for the goddamn lights."

"What were you doing with the gun?"

"You *know* what I was doing. I was shooting at the lampposts."

"Did you start out with that idea? Shooting at the lampposts?"

"Yeah. Listen, I don't have to say anything to you. I want a lawyer."

"You'll have plenty opportunity for a lawyer."

"Well, I ain't answering any questions until I get one."

"Who's asking questions? We're trying to find out what possessed you to do a damn fool thing like shooting at light fixtures."

"I was high. What the hell, you never been high?"

"I don't go shooting at lampposts when I'm high," the Chief said.

"Well, I do. That's what makes horse races."

"About the gun."

"Yeah, I knew we'd get down to the gun sooner or later."

"Is it yours?"

"Sure, it's mine."

"Where'd you get it?"

"My brother sent it home to me."

"Where's your brother?"

"In Korea."

"Have you got a permit for the gun?"

"It was a gift."

"I don't give a damn if you *made* it! Have you got a permit?"

"No."

"Then what gave you the idea you could go around carrying it?"

"I just got the idea. Lots of people carry guns. What the hell are you picking on me for? All I shot was a few lights. Why don't you go after the bastards who are shooting people?"

"How do we know you're not one of them, Bronckin?"

"Maybe I am. Maybe I'm Jack the Ripper."

"Maybe not. But maybe you were carrying that .45 and planning a little worse mischief than shooting out a few lights."

"Sure. I was gonna shoot the Mayor."

"A .45," Carella whispered to Bush.

"Yeah," Bush said. He was already out of his chair and walking back to the Chief of Detectives.

"All right, smart guy," the Chief of Detectives said. "You violated the Sullivan Law. Do you know what that means?"

"No, what does it mean, smart guy?"

"You'll find out," the Chief said. "Next case."

At his elbow, Bush said, "Chief, we'd like to question that man further."

"Go ahead," the Chief said. "Hillside, One. Matheson, Peter, 45 . . ."

14

David Bronckin did not appreciate the idea of being detained from his visit to the Criminal Courts Building, whereto he was being led for arraignment when Carella and Bush intercepted him.

He was a tall man, at least six-three, and he had a very loud voice and a very pugnacious attitude, and he didn't like Carella's first request at all.

"Lift your foot," Carella said.

"What?"

The men were seated in the Detective Squad Room at Headquarters, a room quite similar to the room of the same name back at the 87th. A small fan atop one of the filing cabinets did its best to whip up the air, but the room valiantly upheld its attitude of sleazy limpidity.

"Lift your foot," Carella repeated.

"What for?"

"Because I say so," Carella answered tightly.

Bronckin looked at him for a moment and then said, "You take off that badge and I'll . . ."

"I'm not taking it off," Carella said. "Lift your foot."

Bronckin mumbled something and then raised his right foot. Carella held his ankle and Bush looked at the heel.

"Cat's Paw," Bush said.

"You got any other shoes?" Carella asked.

"Sure, I got other shoes."

"Home?"

"Yeah. What's up?"

"How long have you owned that .45?"

"Couple of months now."

"Where were you Sunday night?"

"Listen, I want a lawyer."

"Never mind the lawyer," Bush said. "Answer the question."

"What was the question?"

"Where were you Sunday night?"

"What time Sunday night?"

"About 11:40 or so."

"I think I was at a movie."

"Which movie?"

"The Strand. Yeah, I was at a movie."

"Did you have the .45 with you?"

"I don't remember."

"Yes or no."

"I don't remember. If you want a yes or no, it'll have to be no. I'm no dope."

"What picture did you see?"

"An old one."

"Name it."

"The Creature from the Black Lagoon."

"What was it about?"

"A monster that comes up from the water."

"What was the co-feature?"

"I don't remember."

"Think."

"Something with John Garfield."

"What?"

"A prize-fight picture."

"What was the title?"

"I don't remember. He's a bum, and then he gets to be champ, and then he takes a dive."

"Body and Soul?"

"Yeah, that was it."

"Call the Strand, Hank," Carella said.

"Hey, what're you gonna do that for?" Bronckin asked.

"To check and see if those movies were playing Sunday night."

"They were playing, all right."

"We're also going to check that .45 with Ballistics, Bronckin."

"What for?"

"To see how it matches up against some slugs we've got. You can save us a lot of time."

"How?"

"What were you doing Monday night?"

"Monday, Monday? Jesus, who remembers?"

Bush had located the number in the directory, and was dialing.

"Listen," Bronckin said, "you don't have to call them. Those were the pictures, all right."

"What were you doing Monday night?"

"I . . . I went to a movie."

"Another movie? Two nights in a row?"

"Yeah. The movies are air-conditioned. It's better than hanging around and suffocating, ain't it?"

"What'd you see?"

"Some more old ones."

"You like old movies, don't you?"

"I don't care about the picture. I was only tryin' to beat the heat. The places showing old movies are cheaper."

"What were the pictures?"

"Seven Brides for Seven Brothers and *Violent Saturday."*

"You remember those all right, do you?"

"Sure, it was more recent."

"Why'd you say you couldn't remember what you did Monday night?"

"I said that?"

"Yes."

"Well, I had to think."

"What movie house was this?"

"On Monday night, you mean?"

"Yeah."

"One of the RKO's. The one on North 80th."

Bush put the receiver back into its cradle. "Checks out, Steve," he said. *"Creature from the Black Lagoon,* and *Body and Soul.* Like he said." Bush didn't mention that he'd also taken down a timetable for the theatre, or that he knew exactly what times each picture started and ended. He nodded briefly at Carella, passing on the information.

"What time did you go in?"

"Sunday or Monday?"

"Sunday."

"About 8:30."

"Exactly 8:30?"

"Who remembers exactly? It was getting hot, so I went into the Strand."

"What makes you think it was 8:30?"

"I don't know. It was about that time."

"What time did you leave?"

"About—musta been about a quarter to twelve."

"Where'd you go then?"

"For some coffee and."

"Where?"

"The White Tower."

"How long did you stay?"

"Half-hour, I guess."

"What'd you eat?"

"I told you. Coffee and."

"Coffee and *what*?"

"Jesus, a jelly donut," Bronckin said.

"This took you a half-hour?"

"I had a cigarette while I was there."

"Meet anybody you know there?"

"No."

"At the movie?"

"No."

"And you didn't have the gun with you, that right?"

"I don't think I did."

"Do you usually carry it around?"

"Sometimes."

"You ever been in trouble with the Law?"

"Yeah."

"Spell it."

"I served two at Sing Sing."

"What for?"

"Assault with a deadly weapon."

"What was the weapon?"

Bronckin hesitated.

"I'm listening," Carella said.

"A .45."

"This one?"

"No."

"Which?"

"Another one I had."

"Have you still got it?"

Again, Bronckin hesitated.

"Have you still got it?" Carella repeated.

"Yes."

"How come? Didn't the police . . ."

"I ditched the gun. They never found it. A friend of mine picked it up for me."

"Did you use the business end?"

"No. The butt."

"On who?"

"What difference does it make?"

"I want to know. Who?"

"A . . . a lady."

"A woman?"

"Yes."

"How old?"

"Forty. Fifty."

"Which?"

"Fifty."

"You're a nice guy."

"Yeah," Bronckin said.

"Who collared you? Which precinct?"

"Ninety-second, I think."

"Was it?"

"Yes."

"Who were the cops?"

"I don't know."

"The ones who made the arrest, I mean."

"There was only one."

"A dick?"

"No."

"When was this?" Bush asked.

"Fifty-two."

"Where's that other .45?"

"Back at my room."

"Where?"

"831 Haven."

Carella jotted down the address.

"What else have you got there?"

"You guys going to help me?"

"What help do you need?"

"Well, I keep a few guns."

"How many?"

"Six," Bronckin said.

"What?"

"Yeah."

"Name them."

"The two .45's. Then there's a Luger, and a Mauser, and I even got a Tokarev."

"What else?"

"Oh, just a .22."

"All in your room?"

"Yeah, it's quite a collection."

"Your shoes there, too?"

"Yeah. What's with my shoes?"

"No permits for any of these guns, huh?"

"No. Slipped my mind."

"I'll bet. Hank, call the Ninety-second. Find out who collared Bronckin in '52. I think Foster started at our house, but Reardon may have been a transfer."

"Oh," Bronckin said suddenly.

"What?"

"That's what this is all about, huh? Those two cops."

"Yes."

"You're way off," Bronckin said.

"Maybe. What time'd you get out of that RKO?"

"About the same. Eleven-thirty, twelve."

"The other one check, Hank?"

"Yep."

"Better call the RKO on North 80th and check this one, too. You can go now, Bronckin. Your escort's in the hall."

"Hey," Bronckin said, "how about a break? I helped you, didn't I? How about a break?"

Carella blew his nose.

None of the shoes in Bronckin's apartment owned heels even faintly resembling the heelprint cast the Lab boys had.

Ballistics reported that neither of the .45's in Bronckin's possession could have fired any of the fatal bullets.

The 92nd Precinct reported that neither Michael Reardon or David Foster had ever worked there.

There was only one thing the investigators could bank on.

The heat.

15

At seven twenty-six that Thursday night, the city looked skyward.

The city had heard a sound, and it paused to identify the sound. The sound was the roll of distant thunder.

And it seemed, simultaneously, as if a sudden breeze sprang up from the north and washed the blistering face of the city. The ominous rolling in the sky grew closer, and now there were lightning flashes, erratic, jagged streaks that knifed the sky.

The people of the city turned their faces upward and waited.

It seemed the rain would never come. The lightning was wild in its fury, lashing the tall buildings, arcing over the horizon. The thunder answered the spitting anger of the lightning, booming its own furious epithets.

And then, suddenly, the sky split open and the rain poured down. Huge drops, and they pelted the sidewalks and the gutters and the streets; and the asphalt and concrete sizzled when the first drops fell;

and the citizens of the city smiled and watched the
rain, watched the huge drops—God, how big the
drops were!—splattering against the ground. And
the smiles broadened, and people slapped each
other on the back, and it looked as if everything was
going to be all right again.

Until the rain stopped.

It stopped as suddenly as it had begun. It had burst
from the sky like water that had broken through a
dam. It rained for four minutes and thirty-six seconds. And then, as though someone had suddenly
plugged the broken wall of the dam, it stopped.

The lightning still flashed across the sky, and the
thunder still growled in response, but there was no
rain.

The cool relief the rain had brought lasted no
more than ten minutes. At the end of that time, the
streets were baking again, and the citizens were
swearing and mumbling and sweating.

Nobody likes practical jokes.

Even when God is playing them.

She stood by the window when the rain stopped.

She swore mentally, and she reminded herself
that she would have to teach Steve sign language, so
that he'd know when she was swearing. He had
promised to come tonight, and the promise filled
her now, and she wondered what she should wear
for him.

"Nothing" was probably the best answer. She was
pleased with her joke. She must remember it. To tell
to him when he came.

The street was suddenly very sad. The rain had brought gaiety, but now the rain was gone, and there was only the solemn grey of the street, as solemn as death.

Death.

Two dead, two men he worked with and knew well. Why couldn't he have been a streetcleaner or a flagpole sitter or something, why a policeman, why a cop?

She turned to look at the clock, wondering what time it was, wondering how long it would be before he came, how long it would be before she spotted the slow, back-and-forth twisting of the knob, before she rushed to the door to open it for him. The clock was no comfort. It would be hours yet. If he came, of course. If nothing else happened, something to keep him at the station house, another killing, another . . .

No, I mustn't think of that.

It's not fair to Steve to think that.

If I think of harm coming to him . . .

Nothing will happen to him . . . no. Steve is strong, Steve is a good cop, Steve can take care of himself. But Reardon was a good cop, and Foster, and they're dead now. How good can a cop be when he's shot in the back with a .45? How good is any cop against a killer in ambush?

No, don't think these things.

The murders are over now. There will be no more. Foster was the end. It's done. Done.

Steve, hurry.

She sat facing the door, knowing it would be

hours yet, but waiting for the knob to turn, waiting
for the knob to tell her he was there.

The man rose.

He was in his undershorts. They were gaily pat-
terned, and they fitted him snugly, and he walked
from the bed to the dresser with a curiously ducklike motion. He was a tall man, excellently built. He
examined his profile in the mirror over the dresser,
looked at the clock, sighed heavily, and then went
back to the bed.

There was time yet.

He lay and looked at the ceiling, and then he suddenly desired a cigarette. He rose and walked to the
dresser again, walking with the strange ducklike
waddle which was uncomplimentary to a man of his
physique. He lighted the cigarette and then went
back to the bed, where he lay puffing and thinking.

He was thinking about the cop he would kill later
that night.

Lieutenant Byrnes stopped in to chat with Captain Frick, commanding officer of the precinct, before he checked out that night.

"How's it going?" Frick asked.

Byrnes shrugged. "Looks like we've got the only
cool thing in this city."

"Huh?"

"This case."

"Oh. Yeah," Frick said. Frick was tired. He wasn't
as young as he used to be, and all this hullabaloo
made him tired. If cops got knocked off, those were

the breaks. Here today, gone tomorrow. You can't
live forever, and you can't take it with you. Find the
perpetrator, sure, but don't push a man too hard.
You can't push a man too hard in this heat, especially when he's not as young as he used to be, and
tired.

To tell the truth, Frick was a tired man even when
he was twenty, and Byrnes knew it. He didn't particularly care for the captain, but he was a conscientious cop, and a conscientious cop checked with the
precinct commander every now and then, even if he
felt the commander was an egghead.

"You're really working the boys, aren't you?" Frick
asked.

"Yes," Byrnes said, thinking that should have been
obvious even to an egghead.

"I figure this for some screwball," Frick said. "Got
himself a peeve, figured he'd go out and shoot
somebody."

"Why cops?" Byrnes asked.

"Why not? How can you figure what a screwball
will do? Probably knocked off Reardon by accident,
not even knowing he was a cop. Then saw all the
publicity the thing got in the papers, figured it was
a good idea, and purposely gunned for another
cop."

"How'd he know Foster *was* a cop? Foster was in
street clothes, same as Reardon."

"Maybe he's a screwball who's had run-ins with
the law before, how do I know? One thing's for sure,
though. He's a screwball."

"Or a mighty shrewd guy," Byrnes said.

"How do you figure that? What brains does it take to pull a trigger?"

"It doesn't take any brains," Byrnes said. "Unless you get away with it."

"He won't," Frick answered. He sighed expansively. He was tired. He was getting old. Even his hair was white. Old men shouldn't have to solve mysteries in hot weather.

"Hot, ain't it?" Frick said.

"Yes indeed," Byrnes replied.

"You heading for home now?"

"Yes."

"Good for you. I'll be taking off in a little while, too. Some of the boys are out on an attempted suicide, though. Want to find out how it turns out. Some dame on the roof, supposed to be ready to jump." Frick shook his head. "Screwballs, huh?"

"Yeah," Byrnes said.

"Sent my wife and kids away to the mountains," Frick said. "Damn glad I did. This heat ain't fit for man nor beast."

"No, it's not," Byrnes agreed.

The phone on Frick's desk rang. Frick picked it up.

"Captain Frick," he said. "What? Oh. Okay, fine. Right." He replaced the receiver. "Not a suicide at all," he said to Byrnes. "The dame was just drying her hair, had it sort of hanging over the edge of the roof. Screwball, huh?"

"Yes. Well, I'm taking off."

"Better keep your gun handy. Might get you next."

"Who?" Byrnes asked, heading for the door.

"Him."

"Huh?"

"The screwball."

Roger Havilland was a bull.

Even the other bulls called him a bull. A real bull. He was a "bull" as differentiated from a "bull" which was a detective. Havilland was built like a bull, and he ate like a bull, and he screwed like a bull, and he even snorted like a bull. There were no two ways about it. He was a real bull.

He was also not a very nice guy.

There was a time when Havilland was a nice guy, but everyone had forgotten that time, including Havilland. There was a time when Havilland could talk to a prisoner for hours on end without once having to use his hands. There was a time when Havilland did not bellow every other syllable to leave his mouth. Havilland had once been a gentle cop.

But Havilland had once had a most unfortunate thing happen to him. Havilland had tried to break up a street fight one night, being on his way home at the time and being, at the time, that sort of conscientious cop who recognized his duty twenty-four hours a day. The street fight had not been a very big one, as street fights go. As a matter of fact, it was a friendly sort of argument, more or less, with hardly a zip gun in sight.

Havilland stepped in and very politely attempted to bust it up. He drew his revolver and fired a few shots over the heads of the brawlers and somehow or other one of the brawlers hit Havilland on the right wrist with a piece of lead pipe. The gun left Havilland's hand, and then the unfortunate thing happened.

The brawlers, content until then to be bashing in their own heads, suddenly decided a cop's head would be more fun to play upon. They turned on the disarmed Havilland, dragged him into an alley, and went to work on him with remarkable dispatch.

The boy with the lead pipe broke Havilland's arm in four places.

The compound fracture was a very painful thing to bear, more painful in that the damned thing would not set properly and the doctors were forced to rebreak the bones and set them all over again.

For a while there, Havilland doubted if he'd be able to keep his job on the force. Since he'd only recently made Detective 3rd Grade, the prospect was not a particularly pleasant one to him. But the arm healed, as arms will, and he came out of it just about as whole as he went into it—except that his mental attitude had changed somewhat.

There is an old adage which goes something like this: "One guy can screw it up for the whole company."

Well, the fellow with the lead pipe certainly screwed it up for the whole company, if not the whole city. Havilland became a bull, a real bull. He had learned his lesson. He would never be cornholed again.

In Havilland's book, there was only one way to beat down a prisoner's resistance. You forgot the

word "down," and you concentrated on beating in the opposite direction: "up."

Not many prisoners liked Havilland.

Not many *cops* liked him, either.

It is even doubtful whether or not Havilland liked himself.

"Heat," he said to Carella, "is all in the mind."

"My mind is sweating the same as the rest of me," Carella said.

"If I told you right this minute that you were sitting on a cake of ice in the middle of the Arctic Ocean, you'd begin to feel cool."

"I don't feel any cooler," Carella said.

"That's because you're a jackass," Havilland said, shouting. Havilland always shouted. When Havilland whispered, he shouted. "You don't want to feel cool. You want to feel hot. It makes you think you're working."

"I am working."

"I'm going home," Havilland shouted abruptly.

Carella glanced at his watch. It was 10:17.

"What's the matter?" Havilland shouted.

"Nothing."

"It's a quarter after ten, that's what you're looking sour about?" Havilland bellowed.

"I'm not looking sour."

"Well, I don't care how you look," Havilland roared. "I'm going home."

"So go home. I'm waiting for my relief."

"I don't like the way you said that," Havilland answered.

"Why not?"

"It implied that *I* am *not* waiting for my relief."

Carella shrugged and blithely said, "Let your conscience be your guide, brother."

"Do you know how many hours I've been on this job?"

"How many?"

"Thirty-six," Havilland said. "I'm so sleepy I could crawl into a sewer and not wake up until Christmastime."

"You'll pollute our water supply," Carella said.

"Up yours!" Havilland shouted. He signed out and was leaving when Carella said, "Hey!"

"What?"

"Don't get killed out there."

"Up yours," Havilland said again, and then he left.

The man dressed quietly and rapidly. He put on black trousers and a clean white shirt, and a gold-and-black striped tie. He put on dark blue socks, and then he reached for his shoes. His shoes carried O'Sullivan heels.

He put on the black jacket to his suit, and then he went to the dresser and opened the top drawer. The .45 lay on his handkerchiefs, lethal and blue-black. He pushed a fresh clip into the gun, and then put the gun into his jacket pocket.

He walked to the door in a ducklike waddle, opened it, took a last look around the apartment, flicked out the lights, and went into the night.

Steve Carella was relieved at 11:33 by a detective named Hal Willis. He filled Willis in on anything that was urgent, left him to catch and then walked downstairs.

"Going to see the girlfriend, Steve?" the desk sergeant asked.

"Yep," Carella answered.

"Wish I was as young as you," the sergeant said.

"Ah, come on," Carella replied. "You can't be more than seventy."

The sergeant chuckled. "Not a day over," he answered.

"Good night," Carella said.

"Night."

Carella walked out of the building and headed for his car, which was parked two blocks away in a "No Parking" zone.

Hank Bush left the precinct at 11:52 when his relief showed up.

"I thought you'd never get here," he said.

"I thought so, too."

"What happened?"

"It's too hot to run."

Bush grimaced, went to the phone, and dialed his home number. He waited several moments. The phone kept ringing on the other end.

"Hello?"

"Alice?"

"Yes." She paused. "Hank?"

"I'm on my way, honey. Why don't you make some iced coffee?"

"All right, I will."

"Is it very hot there?"

"Yes. Maybe you should pick up some ice cream."

"All right."

"No, never mind. No. Just come home. The iced coffee will do."

"Okay. I'll see you later."

"Yes, darling."

Bush hung up. He turned to his relief. "I hope you don't get relieved 'til nine, you bastard," he said.

"The heat's gone to his head," the detective said to the air.

Bush snorted, signed out, and left the building.

The man with the .45 waited in the shadows.

His hand sweated on the walnut stock of the .45 in his jacket pocket. Wearing black, he knew he blended with the void of the alley mouth, but he was nonetheless nervous and a little frightened. Still, this had to be done.

He heard footsteps approaching. Long, firm strides. A man in a hurry. He stared up the street. Yes.

Yes, this was his man.

His hand tightened on the .45.

The cop was closer now. The man in black stepped out of the alleyway abruptly. The cop stopped in his tracks. They were almost of the same height. A street lamp on the corner cast their shadows onto the pavement.

"Have you got a light, Mac?"

The cop was staring at the man in black. Then, suddenly, the cop was reaching for his back pocket. The man in black saw what was happening, and he brought up the .45 quickly, wrenching it free from his pocket. Both men fired simultaneously.

He felt the cop's bullet rip into his shoulder, but the .45 was bucking now, again and again, and he saw the cop clutch at his chest and fall for the pavement. The Detective's Special lay several feet from the cop's body now.

He backed away from the cop, ready to run.

"You son of a bitch," the cop said.

He whirled. The cop was on his feet, rushing for him. He brought up the .45 again, but he was too late. The cop had him, his thick arms churning. He fought, pulling free, and the cop clutched at his head, and he felt hair wrench loose, and then the cop's fingers clawed at his face, ripping, gouging.

He fired again. The cop doubled over and then fell to the pavement, his face colliding with the harsh concrete.

His shoulder was bleeding badly. He cursed the cop, and he stood over him, and his blood dripped onto the lifeless shoulders, and he held the .45 out at arm's length and squeezed the trigger again. The cop's head gave a sideward lurch and then was still.

The man in black ran off down the street.

The cop on the sidewalk was Hank Bush.

16

Sam Grossman was a police lieutenant. He was also a lab technician. He was tall and angular, a man who'd have looked more at home on a craggy New England farm than in the sterile orderliness of the Police Laboratory which stretched almost half the length of the first floor at Headquarters.

Grossman wore glasses, and his eyes were a guileless blue behind them. There was a gentility to his manner, a quiet warmth reminiscent of a long-lost era, even though his speech bore the clipped stamp of a man who is used to dealing with cold scientific fact.

"Hank was a smart cop," he said to Carella.

Carella nodded. It was Hank who'd said that it didn't take much brain power to be a detective.

"The way I figure it," Grossman went on, "Hank thought he was a goner. The autopsy disclosed four wounds altogether, three in the chest, one at the back of the head. We can safely assume, I think, that the head shot was the last one fired, a *coup de grâce.*"

"Go ahead," Carella said.

"Figure he'd been shot two or three times already, and possibly knew he'd be a dead pigeon before this was over. Whatever the case, he knew we could use more information on the bastard doing the shooting."

"The hair, you mean?" Carella asked.

"Yes. We found clumps of hair on the sidewalk. All the hairs had living roots, so we'd have known they were pulled away by force even if we hadn't found some in the palms and fingers of Hank's hands. But he was thinking overtime. He also tore a goodly chunk of meat from the ambusher's face. That told us a few things, too."

"And what else?"

"Blood. Hank shot this guy, Steve. Well, undoubtedly you know that already."

"Yes. What does it all add up to?"

"A lot," Grossman said. He picked up a report from his desk. "This is what we know for sure, from what we were able to piece together, from what Hank gave us."

Grossman cleared his throat and began reading.

"The killer is a male, white, adult, not over say fifty years of age. He is a mechanic, possibly highly skilled and highly paid. He is dark complected, his skin is oily, he has a heavy beard which he tries to disguise with talc. His hair is dark brown, and he is approximately six feet tall. Within the past two days, he took a haircut and a singe. He is fast, possibly indicating a man who is not overweight. Judging from the hair, he should weigh about 180. He is wounded, most likely above the waist, and not superficially."

"Break it down for me," Carella said, somewhat amazed—as he always was—by what the Lab boys could do with a rag, a bone, and a hank of hair.

"Okay," Grossman said. "Male. In this day and age, this sometimes poses a problem, especially if we've got only hair from the head. Luckily, Hank solved that one for us. The *head* hairs of either a male or a female will have an average diameter of less than 0.08 mm. Okay, having only a batch of head hairs to go on, we've got to resort to other measurements to determine whether or not the hair came from a male or a female. Length of the hair used to be a good gauge. If the length was more than 8 cm., we could assume the hair came from a woman. But the goddamn women nowadays are wearing their hair as short as, if not shorter than, the men. So we could have been fooled on this one, if Hank hadn't scratched this guy's face."

"What's the scratch have to do with it?"

"It gave us a skin sample, to begin with. That's how we knew the man was white, dark complected, and oily. But it also gave us a beard hair."

"How do you know it was a beard hair?"

"Simple," Grossman said. "Under the microscope, it showed up in cross-section as being triangular, with concave sides. Only beard hairs are shaped that way. The diameter, too, was greater than 0.1 mm. Simple. A beard hair. Had to be a man."

"How do you know he was a mechanic?"

"The head hairs were covered with metal dust."

"You said possibly a highly skilled and highly paid one. Why?"

"The head hairs were saturated with a hair preparation. We broke it down and checked it against our sample sheets. It's very expensive stuff. Five bucks the bottle when sold singly. Ten bucks when sold in a set with the after-shave talc. This customer was wearing both the hair gook *and* the talc. What mechanic can afford ten bucks for such luxuries—unless he's highly paid? If he's highly paid, chances are he's highly skilled."

"How do you know he's not over fifty?" Carella asked.

"Again, by the diameter of the hair and also the pigmentation. Here, take a look at this chart." He extended a sheet to Carella.

Age	Diameter
12 days	0.024 mm.
6 months	0.037 mm.
18 months	0.038 mm.
15 years	0.053 mm.
Adults	0.07 mm.

"Fellow's head hair had a diameter of 0.071," Grossman said.

"That only shows he's an adult."

"Sure. But if we get a hair with a living root, and there are hardly any pigment grains in the cortex, we can be pretty sure the hair comes from an old person. This guy had plenty of pigment grains. Also, even though we rarely make any age guesses on such single evidence, an older person's hair has a tendency to become finer. This guy's hair is coarse and thick."

Carella sighed.

"Am I going too fast for you?"

"No," Carella said. "How about the singe and the haircut?"

"The singe was simple. The hairs were curled, slightly swelled, and greyish in color. Not naturally grey, you understand."

"The haircut?"

"If the guy had had a haircut just before he did the shooting, the head hairs would have shown clean-cut edges. After forty-eight hours, the cut begins to grow round. We can pretty well determine just when a guy's had his last haircut."

"You said he was six feet tall."

"Well, Ballistics helped us on that one."

"Spell it," Carella said.

"We had the blood to work with. Did I mention the guy has type O blood?"

"You guys . . ." Carella started.

"Aw come on, Steve, that was simple."

"Yeah."

"Yeah," Grossman said. "Look, Steve, the blood serum of one person has the ability to agglutinate . . ." He paused. "That means clump, or bring together the red blood cells of certain other people. There are four blood groups: Group O, Group A, Group B, Group AB. Okay?"

"Okay," Carella said.

"We take the sample of blood, and we mix a little of it with samples from the four groups. Oh, hell, here's another chart for you to look at." He handed it to Carella.

1. Group O —no agglutination in either
serum.
2. Group A —agglutination in serum B only.
3. Group B —agglutination in serum A only.
4. Group AB —agglutination in both serums.

"This guy's blood—and he left a nice trail of it when he was running away, in addition to several spots on the back of Hank's shirt—would not agglutinate, or clump, in any of the samples. Hence, type O. Another indication that he's white, incidentally. A and O are most common in white people; 45 percent of all white people are in the O group."

"How do you figure he's six feet tall? You still haven't told me."

"Well, as I said, this is where Ballistics came in. In addition to what we had, of course. The blood spots on Hank's shirt weren't of much value in determining from what height they had fallen since the cotton absorbed them when they hit. But the bloodstains on the pavement told us several things."

"What'd they tell you?"

"First that he was going pretty fast. You see, the faster a man is walking, the narrower and longer will be the blood drops and the teeth on those drops. They look something like a small gear, if you can picture that, Steve."

"I can."

"Okay. These were narrow and also sprinkled in many small drops, which told us that he was moving fast and also that the drops were falling from a height of somewhere around two yards or so."

"So?"

"So, if he was moving fast, he wasn't hit in the legs or the stomach. A man doesn't move very fast under those conditions. If the drops came from a height of approximately two yards, chances are the man was hit high above the waist. Ballistics pried Hank's slug out of the brick wall of the building, and from the angle—assuming Hank only had time to shoot from a draw—they figured the man was struck somewhere around the shoulder. This indicates a tall man, I mean when you put the blood drops and the slug together."

"How do you know he wasn't wounded superficially?"

"All the blood, man. He left a long trail."

"You said he weighs about 180. How . . ."

"The hair was healthy hair. The guy was going fast. The speed tells us he wasn't overweight. A healthy man of six feet should weigh about 180, no?"

"You've given me a lot, Sam," Carella said. "Thanks."

"Don't mention it. I'm glad I'm not the guy who has to check on doctors' gunshot wound reports, or absentee mechanics. Not to mention this hair lotion and talc. It's called 'Skylark,' by the way."

"Well, thanks, anyway."

"Don't thank me," Grossman said.

"Huh?"

"Thank Hank."

17

The teletype alarm went out to fourteen states. It read:

XXXXX APPREHEND SUSPICION OF MURDER XXX UNIDENTIFIED MALE WHITE CAUCASIAN ADULT BELOW FIFTY XXXXX POSSIBLE HEIGHT SIX FEET OR OVER XXX POSSIBLE WEIGHT ONE HUNDRED EIGHTY XXX DARK HAIR SWARTHY COMPLEXION HEAVY BEARD XXXX USES HAIR PREPARATION AND TALC TRADENAME "SKYLARK" XXXX SHOES MAY POSSIBLY CARRY HEELS WITH "O'SULLIVAN" TRADENAME XXXX MAN ASSUMED TO BE SKILLED MECHANIC MAY POSSIBLY SEEK SUCH WORK XXXXX GUNWOUND ABOVE WAIST POSSIBLE SHOULDER HIGH MAN MAY SEEK DOCTOR XXXX THIS MAN IS DANGEROUS AND ARMED WITH COLT .45 AUTOMATIC XX

"Those are a lot of 'possiblys'," Havilland said.

"Too damn many," Carella agreed. "But at least it's a place to start."

It was not so easy to start.

They could, of course, have started by calling all the doctors in the city, on the assumption that one or more of them had failed to report a gunshot wound, as specified by law. However, there were quite a few doctors in the city. To be exact, there were:

> 4,283 doctors in Calm's Point
> 1,975 doctors in Riverhead
> 8,728 doctors in Isola (including the
>   Diamondback and Hillside sectors)
> 2,614 doctors in Majesta and
>   264 doctors in Bethtown for a grand total of
>   COUNT 'EM!
> 17,864 DOCTORS 17,864

Those are a lot of medical men. Assuming each call would take approximately five minutes, a little multiplication told the cops it would take them approximately 89,320 minutes to call each doctor in the classified directory. Of course, there were 22,000 policemen on the force. If each cop took on the job of calling four doctors, every call could have been made before twenty minutes had expired. Unfortunately, many of the other cops had other tidbits of crime to occupy themselves with. So, faced with the overwhelming number of healers, the detectives decided to wait—instead—for one of them to call with a gunshot wound report. Since the bullet had exited the killer's body, the wound was in all likelihood a clean one, anyway, and perhaps the killer would *never* seek the aid of a doctor. In which case the waiting would all be in vain.

If there were 17,864 doctors in the city, it was virtually impossible to tally the number of mechanics plying their trade there. So this line of approach was also abandoned.

There remained the hair lotion and talc with the innocent-sounding name "Skylark."

A quick check showed that both masculine beauty aids were sold over the counter of almost every drugstore in the city. They were as common as—if higher-priced than—aspirin tablets.

Good for a cold.

If you don't like them . . .

The police turned, instead, to their own files in the Bureau of Identification, and to the voluminous files in the Federal Bureau of Investigation.

And the search was on for a male, white Caucasian, under fifty years in age, dark haired, dark complected, six feet tall, weighing one hundred eighty pounds, addicted to the use of a Colt .45 automatic.

The needle may have been in the city.

But the entire United States was the haystack.

"Lady to see you, Steve," Miscolo said.

"What about?"

"Said she wanted to talk to the people investigating the cop killer." Miscolo wiped his brow. There was a big fan in the Clerical office, and he hated leaving it. Not that he didn't enjoy talking to the DD men. It was simply that Miscolo was a heavy sweater, and he didn't like the armpits of his uniform shirts ruined by unnecessary talk.

"Okay, send her in," Carella said.

Miscolo vanished, and then reappeared with a small birdlike woman whose head jerked in short arcs as she surveyed first the dividing railing and then the file cabinets and then the desks and the grilled windows and then the detectives on phones everywhere in the squad room, most of them in various stages of sartorial inelegance.

"This is Detective Carella," Miscolo said. "He's one of the detectives on the investigation." Miscolo sighed heavily and then fled back to the big fan in the small Clerical office.

"Won't you come in, ma'm?" Carella said.

"*Miss,*" the woman corrected. Carella was in his shirtsleeves, and she noticed this with obvious distaste, and then glanced sharply around the room again and said, "Don't you have a private office?"

"I'm afraid not," Carella said.

"I don't want them to hear me."

"Who?" Carella asked.

"Them," she said. "Could we go to a desk somewhere in the corner?"

"Certainly," Carella said. "What did you say your name was, Miss?"

"Oreatha Bailey," the woman said. She was at least fifty-five or so, Carella surmised, with the sharp-featured face of a stereotyped witch. He led her through the gate in the railing and to an unoccupied desk in the far right corner of the room, a corner which—unfortunately—did not receive any ventilation from the windows.

When they were seated, Carella asked, "What can I do for you, Miss Bailey?"

"You don't have a bug in this corner, do you?"

"A . . . bug?"

"One of them dictaphone things."

"No."

"What did you say your name was?"

"Detective Carella."

"And you speak English?"

Carella suppressed a smile. "Yes, I . . . I picked up the language from the natives."

"I'd have preferred an American policeman," Miss Bailey said in all seriousness.

"Well, I sometimes pass for one," Carella answered, amused.

"Very well."

There was a long pause. Carella waited.

Miss Bailey showed no signs of continuing the conversation.

"Miss . . . ?"

"Shh!" she said sharply.

Carella waited.

After several moments, the woman said, "I know who killed those policemen."

Carella leaned forward, interested. The best leads sometimes came from the most unexpected sources. "Who?" he asked.

"Never you mind," she answered.

Carella waited.

"They are going to kill a lot more policemen," Miss Bailey said. "That's their plan."

"Whose plan?"

"If they can do away with law enforcement, the rest will be easy," Miss Bailey said. "That's their plan. First the police, then the National Guard, and then the regular Army."

Carella looked at Miss Bailey suspiciously.

"They've been sending messages to me," Miss Bailey said. "They think I'm one of them, I don't know why. They come out of the walls and give me messages."

"Who comes out of the walls?" Carella asked.

"The cockroach-men. That's why I asked if there was a bug in this corner."

"Oh, the . . . cockroach-men."

"Yes."

"I see."

"Do I look like a cockroach?" she asked.

"No," Carella said. "Not particularly."

"Then why have they mistaken me for one of them? They look like cockroaches, you know."

"Yes, I know."

"They talk by radio-nuclear-thermics. I think they must be from another planet, don't you?"

"Possibly," Carella said.

"It's remarkable that I can understand them. Perhaps they've overcome my mind. Do you think that's possible?"

"Anything's possible," Carella agreed.

"They told me about Reardon the night before they killed him. They said they would start with him because he was the Commissar of Sector Three.

They used a thermo-disintegrator on him, you know that, don't you?" Miss Bailey paused, and then nodded. ".45 caliber."

"Yes," Carella said.

"Foster was the Black Prince of Argaddon. They had to get him. That's what they told me. The signals they put out are remarkably clear, considering the fact that they're in an alien tongue. I do wish you were an American, Mr. Carella. There are so many aliens around these days, that one hardly knows who to trust."

"Yes," Carella said. He could feel the sweat blotting the back of his shirt. "Yes."

"They killed Bush because he wasn't a bush, he was a tree in disguise. They hate all plant life."

"I see."

"Especially trees. They need the carbon dioxide, you see, and plants consume it. Especially trees. Trees consume a great deal of carbon dioxide."

"Certainly."

"Will you stop them, now that you know?" Miss Bailey asked.

"We'll do everything in our power," Carella said.

"The best way to stop them . . ." Miss Bailey paused and rose, clutching her purse to her narrow bosom. "Well, I don't want to tell you how to run your business."

"We appreciate your help," Carella said. He began walking her to the railing. Miss Bailey stopped.

"Would you like to know the best way to stop these cockroach-men? Guns are no good against them, you know. Because of the thermal heat."

"I didn't know that," Carella said. They were standing just inside the railing. He opened the gate for her, and she stepped through.

"There's only one way to stop them," she said.

"What's that?" Carella asked.

Miss Bailey pursed her mouth. "Step on them!" she said, and she turned on her heel and walked past Clerical, and then down the steps to the first floor.

Bert Kling seemed to be in high spirits that night.

When Carella and Havilland came into the hospital room, he was sitting up in bed, and aside from the bulky bandage over his right shoulder, you'd never know anything was wrong with him. He beamed a broad smile, and then sat up to talk to the two visiting detectives.

He chewed on the candy they'd brought him, and he said this hospital duty was real jazzy, and that they should get a look at some of the nurses in their tight white uniforms.

He seemed to bear no grudge whatever against the boy who'd shot him. Those breaks were all part of the game, he supposed. He kept chewing candy, and joking, and talking until it was almost time for the cops to leave.

Just before they left, he told a joke about a man who had three testicles.

Bert Kling seemed to be in high spirits that night.

18

The three funerals followed upon each other's heels with remarkable rapidity. The heat did not help the classical ceremonies of death. The mourners followed the caskets and sweated. An evil, leering sun grinned its blistering grin, and freshly turned soil—which should have been cool and moist—accepted the caskets with dry, dusty indifference.

The beaches that week were jammed to capacity. In Calm's Point at Mott's Island, the scorekeeper recorded a record-breaking crowd of two million four hundred and seventy thousand surf seekers. The police had problems. The police had traffic problems because everyone who owned any sort of a jalopy had put it on the road. The police had fire-hydrant problems, because kids all over the city were turning on the johnny pumps, covering the spout with a flattened coffee can, and romping beneath the improvised shower. The police had burglary problems, because people were sleeping with their windows open; people were leaving parked cars unlocked, windows wide; shopkeepers were stepping across the street for a moment to catch a quick Pepsi Cola. The police had "floater" problems, because the scorched and heat-weary citizens sometimes sought relief in the polluted currents of the rivers that bound Isola—and some of them drowned, and some of them turned up with bloated bodies and bulging eyes.

On Walker Island, in the River Dix, the police had prisoner problems because the cons there decided the heat was too much for them to bear, and they banged their tin cups on the sweating bars of their hot cells, and the cops listened to the clamor and rushed for riot guns.

The polilce had all sorts of problems.

Carella wished she were not wearing black.

He knew this was absurd. When a woman's husband is dead, the woman wears black.

But Hank and he had talked a lot in the quiet hours of the midnight tour, and Hank had many times described Alice in the black nightgowns she wore to bed. And try as he might, Carella could not disassociate the separate concepts of black: black as a sheer and frothy raiment of seduction; black as the ashy garment of mourning.

Alice Bush sat across from him in the living room of the Calm's Point apartment. The windows were wide open, and he could see the tall Gothic structures of the Calm's Point College campus etched against the merciless, glaring blue of the sky. He had worked with Bush for many years, but this was the first time he'd been inside his apartment, and the association of Alice Bush in black cast a feeling of guilt over his memories of Hank.

The apartment was not at all what he would have expected for a man like Hank. Hank was big, rough-hewn. The apartment was somehow frilly, a woman's apartment. He could not believe that Hank had been comfortable in these rooms. His eyes had scanned the furniture, small-scaled stuff, stuff in which Hank could never have spread his legs. The curtains at the windows were ruffled chintz. The walls of the living room were a sickeningly pale lemon shade. The end tables were heavy with curly-cues and inlaid patterns. The corners of the room contained knick-knack shelves, and the shelves were loaded with fragile glass figurines of dogs and cats and gnomes and one of Little Bo Peep holding a delicately blown, slender glass shepherd's crook.

The room, the apartment, seemed to Carella to be the intricately cluttered design for a comedy of manners. Hank must have been as out of place here as a plumber at a literary tea.

Not so Mrs. Bush.

Mrs. Bush lounged on a heavily padded char-treuse love seat, her long legs tucked under her, her feet bare. Mrs. Bush belonged in this room. This room had been designed for Mrs. Bush, designed for femininity, and the Male Animal be damned.

She wore black silk. She was uncommonly big-busted, incredibly narrow-waisted. Her hip bones were wide, flesh-padded, a woman whose body had been designed for the bearing of children—but somehow she didn't seem the type. He could not visualize her squeezing life from her loins. He could only visualize her as Hank had described her—in the role of a seductress. The black silk dress strengthened the concept. The frou-frou room left no doubt. This was a stage set for Alice Bush.

The dress was not low-cut. It didn't have to be.

Nor was it particularly tight, and it didn't have to be that, either.

It was not expensive, but it fitted her figure well. He had no doubt that anything she wore would fit her figure well. He had no doubt that even a potato sack would look remarkably interesting on the woman who had been Hank's wife.

"What do I do now?" Alice asked. "Make up beds at the precinct? That's the usual routine for a cop's widow, isn't it?"

"Did Hank leave any insurance?" Carella asked.

"Nothing to speak of. Insurance doesn't come easily to cops, does it? Besides . . . Steve, he was a young man. Who thinks of things like this? Who thinks these things are going to happen?" She looked at him wide-eyed. Her eyes were very brown, her hair was very blond, her complexion was fair and unmarred. She was a beautiful woman, and he did not like considering her such. He wanted her to be dowdy and forlorn. He did not want her looking fresh and lovely. Goddamnit, what was there about this room that suffocated a man? He felt like the last male alive, surrounded by bare-breasted beauties on a tropical island surrounded by man-eating sharks. There was no place to run to. The island was called Amazonia or something, and the island was female to the core, and he was the last man alive.

The room and Alice Bush.

The femaleness reached out to envelop him in a cloying, clinging embrace.

"Change your mind, Steve," Alice said. "Have a drink."

"All right, I will," he answered.

She rose, displaying a long white segment of thigh as she got to her feet, displaying an almost indecent oblivion to the way she handled her body. She had lived with it for a long time, he supposed. She no longer marveled at its allure. She accepted it, and lived with it, and others could marvel. A thigh was a thigh, what the hell! What was so special about the thigh of Alice Bush?

"Scotch?"

"All right."

"How does it feel, something like this?" she asked. She was standing at the bar across from him. She stood with the loose-hipped stance of a fashion model, incongruous because he always pictured fashion models as willowy and thin and flat-chested. Alice Bush was none of these.

"Something like what?"

"Investigating the death of a colleague and friend."

"Weird," Carella said.

"I'll bet."

"You're taking it very well," Carella said.

"I have to," Alice answered briefly.

"Why?"

"Because I'll fall all to pieces if I don't. He's in the ground, Steve. It's not going to help for me to wail and moan all over the place."

"I suppose not."

"We've got to go on living, don't we? We can't simply give up because someone we love is gone, can we?"

"No," Carella agreed.

She walked to him and handed him the drink. Their fingers touched for an instant. He looked up at her. Her face was completely guileless. The contact, he was sure, had been accidental.

She walked to the window and looked out toward the college. "It's lonely here without him," she said.

"It's lonely at the house without him, too," Carella said, surprised. He had not realized, before this, how really attached he had become to Hank.

"I was thinking of taking a trip," Alice said, "getting away from things that remind me of him."

"Things like what?" Carella asked.

"Oh, I don't know," Alice said. "Like . . . last night I saw his hairbrush on the dresser, and there was some of that wild red hair of his caught in the bristles, and all at once it reminded me of him, of the wildness of him. He was a wild person, Steve." She paused. "Wild."

The word was female somehow. He was reminded again of the word portrait Hank had drawn, of the real portrait before him, standing by the window, of the femaleness everywhere around him on this island. He could not blame her, he knew that. She was only being herself, being Alice Bush, being Woman.

She was only a pawn of fate, a girl who automatically embodied womanhood, a girl who . . . hell!

"How far have you come along on it?" she asked. She whirled from the window, went back to the love seat and collapsed into it. The movement was not a gracious one. It was feline, however. She sprawled in the love seat like a big jungle cat, and then she tucked her legs under her again, and he would not have been surprised if she'd begun purring in that moment.

He told her what they thought they knew about the suspected killer. Alice nodded.

"Quite a bit to go on," she said.

"Not really."

"I mean, if he should seek a doctor's aid."

"He hasn't yet. Chances are he won't. He probably dressed the wound himself."

"Badly shot?"

"Apparently. But clean."

"Hank should have killed him," she said. Surprisingly, there was no viciousness attached to the words. The words themselves bore all the lethal potential of a coiled rattler, but the delivery made them harmless.

"Yes," Carella agreed. "He should have."

"But he didn't."

"No."

"What's your next step?" she asked.

"Oh, I don't know. Homicide North is up a tree on these killings, and I guess we are, too. I've got a few ideas kicking around, though."

"A lead?" she asked.

"No. Just ideas."

"What kind of ideas?"

"They'd bore you."

"My husband's been killed," Alice said coldly. "I assure you I will not be bored by anything that may lead to finding his killer."

"Well, I'd prefer not to air any ideas until I know what I'm talking about."

Alice smiled. "That's different. You haven't touched your drink."

He raised the glass to his lips. The drink was very strong.

"Wow!" he said. "You don't spare the alcohol, do you?"

"Hank liked his strong," she said. "He liked everything strong."

And again, like an interwoven thread of personality, a personality dictated by the demands of a body that could look nothing but blatantly inviting, Alice Bush had inadvertently lit another fuse. He had the feeling that she would suddenly explode into a thousand flying fragments of breast and hip and thigh, splashed over the landscape like a Dali painting.

"I'd better be getting along," he said. "The City doesn't pay me for sipping drinks all morning."

"Stay a while," she said. "I have a few ideas myself."

He glanced up quickly, almost suspecting an edge of double entendre in her voice. He was mistaken. She had turned away from him and was looking out the window again, her face in profile, her body in profile.

"Let me hear them," he said.

"A cop hater," she replied.

"Maybe."

"It has to be. Who else would senselessly take three lives? It has to be a cop hater, Steve. Doesn't Homicide North think so?"

"I haven't talked to them in the past few days. That's what they thought in the beginning, I know."

"What do they think now?"

"That's hard to say."

"What do *you* think now?"

"Maybe a cop hater. Reardon and Foster, yes, a cop hater. But Hank . . . I don't know."

"I'm not sure I follow you."

"Well, Reardon and Foster were partners, so we could assume that possibly some jerk was carrying a grudge against them. They worked together . . . maybe they rubbed some idiot the wrong way."

"Yes?"

"But Hank *never* worked with them. Oh, well maybe not never. Maybe once or twice on a plant or something. He never made an important arrest with either of them along, though. Our records show that."

"Who says it has to be someone with a personal grudge, Steve? This may simply be some goddamned lunatic." She seemed to be getting angry. He didn't know why she was getting angry because she'd certainly been calm enough up to this point. But her breath was coming heavier now, and her breasts heaved disconcertingly. "Just some crazy, rotten, twisted fool who's taken it into his mind to knock off every cop in the 87th Precinct. Does that sound so far-fetched?"

"No, not at all. As a matter of fact, we've checked all the mental institutions in the area for people who were recently released who might possibly have had a history of . . ." He shook his head. "You know, we figured perhaps a paranoiac, somebody who'd go berserk at the sight of a uniform. Except these men weren't in uniform."

"No, they weren't. What'd you get?"

"We thought we had one lead. Not anyone with a history of dislike for policemen, but a young man who had a lot of officer trouble in the Army. He was recently released from Bramlook as cured, but that doesn't mean a goddamned thing. We checked with the psychiatrists there, and they felt his illness would never break out in an act of violence, no less a prolonged rampage of violence."

"And you let it drop?"

"No, we looked the kid up. Harmless. Alibis a mile long."

"Who else have you checked?"

"We've got feelers out to all our underworld contacts. We thought this might be a gang thing, where some hood has an alleged grievance against something we've done to hamper him, and so he's trying to show us we're not so high and mighty. He hires a torpedo and begins methodically putting us in our places. But there's been no rumble so far, and underworld revenge is not something you can keep very quiet."

"What else?"

"I've been wading through F.B.I. photos all morning. Jesus, you'd never realize how many men there are who fit the possible description we have." He sipped at the scotch. He was beginning to feel a little more comfortable with Alice. Maybe she wasn't so female after all. Or maybe her femaleness simply enveloped you after a while, causing you to lose all perspective. Whatever it was, the room wasn't as oppressive now.

"Turn up anything? From the photos?"

"Not yet. Half of them are in jail, and the rest are scattered all over the country. You see, the hell of this thing is . . . well . . ."

"What?"

"How'd the killer know that these men were cops? They were all in plainclothes. Unless he'd had contact with them before, how could he know?"

"Yes, I see what you mean."

"Maybe he sat in a parked car across from the house and watched everyone who went in and out. If he did that for a while, he'd get to know who worked there and who didn't."

"He could have done that," Alice said thoughtfully. "Yes, he could have." She crossed her legs unconsciously. Carella looked away.

"Several things against that theory, though," Carella said. "That's what makes this case such a bitch." The word had sneaked out, and he glanced up apprehensively. Alice Bush seemed not to mind the profanity. She had probably heard enough of it from Hank. Her legs were still crossed. They were very good legs. Her skirt had fallen into a funny position. He looked away again.

"You see, if somebody had been watching the

house, we'd have noticed him. That is, if he'd been watching it long enough to know who worked there and who was visiting . . . that would take time. We'd surely have spotted him."

"Not if he were hidden."

"There are no buildings opposite the house. Only the park."

"He could have been somewhere in the park . . . with binoculars, maybe."

"Sure. But how could he tell the detectives from the patrolmen, then?"

"What?"

"He killed three detectives. Maybe it was chance. I don't think so. All right, how the hell could he tell the patrolmen from the detectives?"

"Very simply," Alice said. "Assuming he was watching, he'd see the men when they arrived, and he'd see them after muster when they went out to their beats. They'd be in uniform then. I'm talking about the patrolmen."

"Yes, I suppose." He took a deep swallow of the drink. Alice moved on the love seat.

"I'm hot," she said.

He did not look at her. He knew that his eyes would have been drawn downward if he did, and he did not want to see what Alice was unconsciously, obliviously showing.

"I don't suppose this heat has helped the investigation any," she said.

"This heat hasn't helped *anything* any."

"I'm changing to shorts and a halter as soon as you get out of here."

"There's a hint if ever I heard one," Carella said.

"No, I didn't mean . . . oh hell, Steve, I'd change to them now if I thought you were going to stay longer. I just thought you were leaving soon. I mean . . ." She made a vague motion with one hand. "Oh, nuts."

"I *am* leaving, Alice. Lots of photos to look through back there." He rose. "Thanks for the drink." He started for the door, not looking back when she got up, not wanting to look at her legs again.

She took his hand at the door. Her grip was firm and warm. Her hand was fleshy. She squeezed his hand.

"Good luck, Steve. If there's anything I can do to help . . ."

"We'll let you know. Thanks again."

He left the apartment and walked down to the street. It was very hot in the street.

Curiously, he felt like going to bed with somebody.

Anybody.

19

"**N**ow here's what I call a real handsome one," Hal Willis said. Hal Willis was the only really small detective Carella had ever known. He passed the minimum height requirement of five-eight, of course, but just barely. And contrasted against the imposing bulk of the other bulls in the division, he looked more like a soft shoe dancer than a tough cop. That he was a tough cop, there was no doubt. His bones were slight, and his face was thin, and he looked as if he would have trouble swatting a fly, but anyone who'd ever tangled with Hal Willis did not want the dubious pleasure again. Hal Willis was a Judo expert.

Hal Willis could shake your hand and break your backbone in one and the same motion. Were you not careful with Hal Willis, you might find yourself enwrapped in the excruciating pain of a Thumb Grip. Were you even less careful, you might discover yourself hurtling through space in the fury of either a Rugby or a Far-Eastern Capsize. Ankle Throws, Flying Mares, Back Wheels, all were as much a part of

Hal Willis' personality as the sparkling brown eyes in his face.

Those eyes were amusedly turned now toward the F.B.I. photo which he shoved across the desk toward Carella.

The photo was of a man who was indeed a "real handsome one." His nose had been fractured in at least four places. A scar ran the length of his left cheek. Scar tissue hooded his eyes. He owned cauliflower ears and hardly any teeth. His name, of course, was "Pretty-Boy Krajak."

"A doll," Carella said. "Why'd they send him to us?"

"Dark hair, six feet two, weighing one-eighty-five. How'd you like to run across him some dark and lonely night?"

"I wouldn't. Is he in the city?"

"He's in L.A.," Willis said.

"Then we'll leave him to Joe Friday," Carella cracked.

"Have another Chesterfield," Willis countered. "The only living cigarette with 60,000 filter dragnets."

Carella laughed. The phone rang. Willis picked it up.

"87th Squad," he said. "Detective Willis."

Carella looked up.

"What?" Willis said. "Give me the address." He scribbled something hastily on his pad. "Hold him there, we'll be right over." He hung up, opened the desk drawer and removed his holster and service revolver.

"What is it?" Carella asked.

"Doctor on 35th North. Has a man in his office with a bullet wound in his left shoulder."

A squad car was parked in front of the brownstone on 35th North when Carella and Willis arrived.

"The rookies beat us here," Willis said.

"So long as they've got him," Carella answered, and he made it sound like a prayer. A sign on the door read: DOCTOR IS IN. RING BELL AND PLEASE BE SEATED.

"Where?" Willis asked. "On the doorstep?"

They rang the bell, opened the door, and entered the office. The office was situated off the small courtyard on the street level of the brownstone. A patrolman was seated on the long leather couch, reading a copy of *Esquire.* He closed the magazine when the detectives entered and said, "Patrolman Curtis, sir."

"Where's the doctor?" Carella asked.

"Inside, sir. Country is asking him some questions."

"Who's Country?"

"My partner, sir."

"Come on," Willis said. He and Carella went into the doctor's office. Country, a tall, gangling boy with a shock of black hair snapped to attention when they entered.

"Goodbye, Country," Willis said dryly. The patrolman eased himself toward the door and left the office.

"Dr. Russell?" Willis asked.

"Yes," Dr. Russell replied. He was a man of about fifty, with a head of hair that was silvery white, giving the lie to his age. He stood as straight as a telephone pole, broad-shouldered, immaculate in his white office tunic. He was a handsome man, and he gave an impression of great competence. For all Carella knew, he may have been a butcher, but he'd have trusted this man to cut out his heart.

"Where is he?"

"Gone," Dr. Russell said.

"How . . ."

"I called as soon as I saw the wound. I excused myself, went out to my private office and placed the call. When I came back, he was gone."

"Shit," Willis said. "Want to tell us from the beginning, Doctor?"

"Certainly. He came in . . . oh, not more than twenty minutes ago. The office was empty, unusual for this time of day, but I rather imagine people with minor ailments are curing them at the seashore." He smiled briefly. "He said he'd shot himself while cleaning his hunting rifle. I took him into the Examination Room—that's *this* room, gentlemen—and asked him to take off his shirt. He did."

"What happened then?"

"I examined the wound. I asked him when he had had the accident. He said it had occurred only this morning. I knew instantly that he was lying. The wound I was examining was not a fresh one. It was already highly infected. That was when I remembered the newspaper stories."

"About the cop killer?"

"Yes. I recalled having read something about the man having a pistol wound above the waist. That was when I excused myself to call you."

"Was this definitely a gunshot wound?"

"Without a doubt. It had been dressed, but very badly. I didn't examine it very closely, you understand, because I rushed off to make the call. But it seemed to me that iodine had been used as a disinfectant."

"Iodine?"

"Yes."

"But it was infected nonetheless?"

"Oh, definitely. That man is going to have to find another doctor, sooner or later."

"What did he look like?"

"Well, where should I begin?"

"How old?"

"Thirty-five or thereabouts."

"Height?"

"A little over six feet, I should say."

"Weight?"

"About one-ninety."

"Black hair?" Willis asked.

"Yes."

"Color of eyes?"

"Brown."

"Any scars, birthmarks, other identifying characteristics?"

"His face was very badly scratched."

"Did he touch anything in the office?"

"No. Wait, yes."

"What?"

"I had him sit up on the table here. When I began probing the wound, he winced and gripped the stirrups here at the foot of the table."

"This may be a break, Hal," Carella said.

"Jesus, it sounds like one. What was he wearing, Dr. Russell?"

"Black."

"Black suit?"

"Yes."

"What color shirt?"

"White. It was stained over the wound."

"Tie?"

"A striped tie. Gold and black."

"Tie clasp?"

"Yes. Some sort of design on it."

"What kind?"

"A bugle? Something like that."

"Trumpet, hunting horn, horn of plenty?"

"I don't know. I couldn't really identify it. It only stuck in my mind because it was an unusual clasp. I noticed it when he was undressing."

"What color shoes?"

"Black."

"Clean-shaven?"

"Yes. That is, you meant was he wearing a beard?"

"Yes."

"Well then, yes, he was clean-shaven. But he needed a shave."

"Uh-huh. Wearing any rings?"

"None that I noticed."

"Undershirt?"

"No undershirt."

"Can't say I blame him in this heat. Mind if I make a call, Doc?"

"Please help yourself. Do you think he's the man?"

"I hope so," Willis said. "God, I hope so."

When a man is nervous, he perspires—even if the temperature is not hovering somewhere in the nineties.

There are sweat pores on the fingertips, and the stuff they secrete contains 98.5 percent water and 0.5 to 1.5 percent solid material. This solid material breaks down to about one-third of inorganic matter—mainly salt—and two-thirds of organic substances like urea, albumin and formic, butyric and acetic acids. Dust, dirt, grease cling to the secretion from a man's fingertips.

The perspiration, mixed with whatever happens to be clinging to it at the moment, leaves a filmy impression on whatever the man happens to touch.

The suspected killer happened to touch the smooth chromium surfaces of the stirrups in Dr. Russell's office.

The tech crew dusted the latent fingerprints with one of the commercial black powders. The excess powder was allowed to fall on a sheet of paper. The prints were lightly brushed with an ostrich feather. They were then photographed.

There were two good thumbprints, one for each hand where the suspect had pressed down on the top surfaces of the stirrups. There were good second-joint prints for each hand where the suspect had gripped the undersides of the stirrups.

The prints were sent to the Bureau of Identification. A thorough search was made of the files. The search proved fruitless, and the prints were sent to the Federal Bureau of Investigation while the detectives sat back to wait.

In the meantime, a police artist went to see Dr. Russell. Listening to Dr. Russell's description, he began drawing a picture of the suspect. He made changes as Dr. Russell suggested them—"No, the nose is a little too long; yes, that's better. Try to give a little curl to his lip there, yes, yes, that's it"—and he finally came up with a drawing which tallied with Dr. Russell's recollection of the man he had examined. The picture was sent to each metropolitan daily and to each television station in the area, together with a verbal description of the wanted man.

All this while, the detectives waited for the F.B.I. report. They were still waiting the next day.

Willis looked at the drawing on the first page of one of the morning tabloids.

The headline screamed: HAVE YOU SEEN THIS MAN?

"He's not bad-looking," Willis said.

"Pretty-Boy Krajak," Carella said.

"No, I'm serious."

"He may be handsome, but he's a son of a bitch," Carella said. "I hope his arm falls off."

"It very well might," Willis said dryly.

"Where the hell's that F.B.I. report?" Carella asked edgily. He had been answering calls all morning, calls from citizens who reported having seen the killer. Each call had to be checked out, of course, but thus far the man had been seen all over the city at simultaneous times. "I thought those G-men were supposed to be fast."

"They are," Willis said.

"I'm going to check with the lieutenant."

"Go ahead," Willis said.

Carella went to the lieutenant's door. He knocked and Byrnes called, "Come." Carella went into the office. Byrnes was on the phone. He signaled for Carella to stand by. He nodded then and said, "But Harriet, I can't see anything wrong with that."

He listened patiently.

"Yes, but . . ."

Carella walked to the window and stared out at the park.

"No, I can't see any reason for . . ."

Marriage, Carella thought. And then he thought of Teddy. *It'll be different with us.*

"Harriet, let him go," Byrnes said. "He's a good boy, and he won't get into any trouble. Look, take my word for it. For God's sake, it's only an amusement park."

Byrnes sighed patiently.

"All right, then." He listened. "I'm not sure yet, honey. We're waiting for an F.B.I. report. If I'll be home, I'll call you. No, nothing special. It's too damn hot to eat, anyway. Yes, dear, 'bye."

He hung up. Carella came from the window.

"Women," Byrnes said, not disagreeably. "My son wants to go out to Jollyland tonight with some of the boys. She doesn't think he should. Can't see why he wants to go there in the middle of the week. She says she's read newspaper stories about boys getting into fights with other boys at these places. For Pete's sake, it's just an amusement park. The kid is seventeen."

Carella nodded.

"If you're going to watch them every minute, they'll feel like prisoners. Okay, what are the odds on a fight starting a place like that? Larry knows enough to avoid trouble. He's a good kid. You met him, didn't you, Steve?"

"Yes," Carella said. "He seemed very levelheaded."

"Sure, that's what I told Harriet. Ah, what the hell! These women never cut the umbilical cord. We get raised by one woman, and then when we're ripe, we get turned over to another woman."

Carella smiled. "It's a conspiracy," he said.

"Sometimes I think so," Byrnes said. "But what would we do without them, huh?" He shook his head sadly, a man trapped in the labial folds of a society structure.

"Anything from the Feds yet?" Carella asked.

"No, not yet. Jesus, I'm praying for a break."

"Mmmm."

"We deserve a break, don't we?" Byrnes asked. "We've worked this one right into the ground. We deserve a break."

There was a knock on the door.

"Come," Byrnes said.

Willis entered the room with an envelope. "This just arrived, sir," he said.

"F.B.I.?"

"Yes."

Byrnes took the envelope. Hastily, he tore open the flap and pulled out the folded letter.

"Hell!" he erupted. "Hell and damnation!"

"Bad?"

"They've got nothing on him!" Byrnes shouted. "Goddamnit! Goddamnit to hell!"

"Not even Service prints?"

"Nothing. The son of a bitch was probably 4-F!"

"We know *everything* about this guy," Willis said vehemently, beginning to pace the office. "We know what he looks like, we know his height, his weight, his blood type, when he got his last haircut, the size of his rectal aperture!" He slammed his fist into the opposite hand. "The only thing we don't know is who the hell he is! Who is he, damnit, who is he?"

Neither Carella nor Byrnes answered.

That night, a boy named Miguel Aretta was taken to Juvenile House. The police had picked him up as one of the boys who'd been missing from the roundup of The Grovers. It did not take the police long to discover that Miguel was the boy who'd zip-gunned Bert Kling.

Miguel had been carrying a zip-gun on the night that Kling got it. When a Senior Grover named Rafael "Rip" Desanga had reported to the boys that a smart guy had been around asking questions, Miguel went with them to teach the smart guy a lesson.

As it turned out, the smart guy—or the person

they assumed to be the smart guy—had pulled a gun outside the bar. Miguel had taken his own piece from his pocket and burned him.

Bert Kling, of course, had not been the smart guy. He turned out to be, of all things, a cop. So Miguel Aretta was now in Juvenile House, and the people there were trying to understand what made him tick so that they could present his case fairly when it came up in Children's Court.

Miguel Aretta was fifteen years old. It could be assumed that he just didn't know any better.

The *real* smart guy—a reporter named Cliff Savage—was thirty-seven years old, and he should have known better.

He didn't.

20

Savage was waiting for Carella when he left the precinct at 4:00 P.M. the next day.

He was wearing a brown Dupioni silk suit, a gold tie, and a brown straw with a pale yellow band. "Hello," he said, shoving himself off the side of the building.

"What can I do for you?" Carella asked.

"You're a detective, aren't you?"

"If you've got a complaint," Carella said, "take it to the desk sergeant. I'm on my way home."

"My name's Savage."

"Oh," Carella said. He regarded the reporter sourly.

"You in the fraternity, too?" Savage asked.

"Which one?"

"The fraternity against Savage. Eeta Piecea Cliff."

"I'm Phi Beta Kappa myself," Carella said.

"Really?"

"No." He began walking toward his car. Savage fell in step with him.

"Are you sore at me, too, is what I meant," Savage said.

"You stuck your nose in the wrong place," Carella answered. "Because you did, a cop is in the hospital and a kid is in Juvenile House, awaiting trial. What do you want me to do, give you a medal?"

"If a kid shoots somebody, he deserves whatever he gets."

"Maybe he wouldn't've shot anybody if you'd kept your nose out of it."

"I'm a reporter. My job is getting facts."

"The lieutenant told me he'd already discussed the possibility of teenagers being responsible for the deaths. He said he told you he considered the possibility extremely remote. But you went ahead and put your fat thumb in the pie, anyway. You realize Kling could have been killed?"

"He wasn't. Do you realize *I* could have been killed?" Savage said.

Carella made no comment.

"If you people cooperated more with the press . . ."

Carella stopped walking. "Listen," he said, "what are you doing in this neighborhood? Looking for more trouble? If any of The Grovers recognize you, we're going to have another rhubarb. Why don't you go back to your newspaper office and write a column on garbage collection?"

"Your humor doesn't . . ."

"I'm not trying to be funny," Carella said, "nor do I particularly feel like discussing anything with you. I just came off duty. I'm going home to shower and then I have a date with my fiancée. I'm theoretically on duty twenty-four hours a day, every day of the week, but fortunately that duty does not include extending courtesy to every stray cub reporter in town."

"Cub?" Savage was truly offended. "Now, listen . . ."

"What the hell do you want from me?" Carella asked.

"I want to discuss the killings."

"I don't."

"Why not?"

"Jesus, you're a real leech, aren't you?"

"I'm a reporter, and a damned good one. Why don't you want to talk about the killings?"

"I'm perfectly willing to discuss them with anyone who knows what I'm talking about."

"I'm a good listener," Savage said.

"Sure. You turned a fine ear toward Rip Desanga."

"Okay, I made a mistake, I'm willing to admit that. I thought it was the kids, and it wasn't. We know now it was an adult. What else do we know about him? Do we know why he did it?"

"Are you going to follow me all the way home?"

"I'd prefer buying you a drink," Savage said. He looked at Carella expectantly. Carella weighed the offer.

"All right," he said.

Savage extended his hand. "My friends call me Cliff. I didn't get your name."

"Steve Carella."

They shook. "Pleased to know you. Let's get that drink."

The bar was air-conditioned, a welcome sanctuary from the stifling heat outdoors. They ordered their drinks and then sat opposite each other at the booth alongside the left-hand wall.

"All I want to know," Savage said, "is what you think."

"Do you mean me personally, or the department?"

"You, of course. I can't expect you to speak for the department."

"Is this for publication?" Carella asked.

"Hell, no. I'm just trying to jell my own ideas on it. Once this thing is broken, there'll be a lot of feature coverage. To do a good job, I want to be acquainted with every facet of the investigation."

"It'd be a little difficult for a layman to understand every facet of police investigation," Carella said.

"Of course, of course. But you can at least tell me what you think."

"Sure. Provided it's not for publication."

"Scout's honor," Savage said.

"The department doesn't like individual cops trying to glorify . . ."

"Not a word of this will get into print," Savage said. "Believe me."

"What do you want to know?"

"We've got the means, we've got the opportunity," Savage said. "What's the motive?"

"Every cop in the city would like the answer to that one," Carella said.

"A nut maybe."

"Maybe."

"You don't think so?"

"No. Some of us do. I don't."

"Why not?"

"Just like that."

"Do you have a reason?"

"No, just a feeling. When you've been working on a case for any length of time, you begin to get feelings about it. I just don't happen to believe a maniac's involved here."

"What *do* you believe?"

"Well, I have a few ideas."

"Like what?"

"I'd rather not say right now."

"Oh, come on, Steve."

"Look, police work is like any other kind of work—except we happen to deal with crime. If you run an import-export business, you play certain hunches and others you don't. It's the same with us. If you have a hunch, you don't go around making a million-dollar deal on it until you've checked it."

"Then you do have a hunch you want to check?"

"Not even a hunch, really. Just an idea."

"What kind of an idea?"

"About motive."

"What about motive?"

Carella smiled. "You're a pretty tenacious guy, aren't you?"

"I'm a good reporter. I already told you that."

"All right, look at it this way. These men were cops. Three of them were killed in a row. What's the automatic conclusion?"

"Somebody doesn't like cops."

"Right. A cop hater."

"So?"

"Take off their uniforms. What have you got then?"

"They weren't wearing uniforms. None of them were uniform cops."

"I know. I was speaking figuratively. I meant, make them ordinary citizens. Not cops. What do you have then? Certainly not a cop hater."

"But they *were* cops."

"They were men first. Cops only coincidentally and secondarily."

"You feel, then, that the fact that they were cops had nothing to do with the reason they were killed."

"Maybe. That's what I want to dig into a little deeper."

"I'm not sure I understand you."

"It's this," Carella said. "We knew these men well, we worked with them every day. Cops. We knew them as cops. We didn't know them as *men*. They may have been killed because they were men, and not because they were cops."

"Interesting," Savage said.

"It means digging into their lives on a more personal level. It won't be fun because murder has a strange way of dragging skeletons out of the neatest closets."

"You mean, for example . . ." Savage paused. "Well,

let's say Reardon was playing around with another dame, or Foster was a horse player, or Bush was taking money from a racketeer, something like that."

"To stretch the point, yes."

"And somehow, their separate activities were perhaps tied together to one person who wanted them all dead for various reasons. Is that what you're saying?"

"That's a little complicated," Carella said. "I'm not sure the deaths are connected in such a complicated way."

"But we do know the same person killed all three cops."

"Yes, we're fairly certain of that."

"Then the deaths are connected."

"Yes, of course. But perhaps . . ." Carella shrugged. "It's difficult to discuss this with you because I'm not sure I know what I'm talking about. I only have this idea, that's all. This idea that motive may go deeper than the shields these men wore."

"I see." Savage sighed. "Well, you can console yourself with the knowledge that every cop in the city probably has his own ideas on how to solve this one."

Carella nodded, not exactly understanding Savage, but not willing to get into a lengthier discussion. He glanced at his watch.

"I've got to go soon," he said. "I've got a date."

"Your girlfriend?"

"Yes."

"What's her name?"

"Teddy. Well, Theodora really."

"Theodora what?"

"Franklin."

"Nice," Savage said. "Is this a serious thing?"

"As serious as they come."

"These ideas of yours," Savage said. "About motive. Have you discussed them with your superiors?"

"Hell, no. You don't discuss every little pang of inspiration you get. You look into it, and then if you turn up anything that looks remotely promising, well, then you air the idea."

"I see. Have you discussed it with Teddy?"

"Teddy? Why, no, not yet."

"Think she'll go for it?"

Carella smiled uneasily. "She thinks I can do no wrong."

"Sounds like a wonderful girl."

"The best. And I'd better get to her before I lose her."

"Certainly," Savage said understandingly. Carella glanced at his watch again. "Where does she live?"

"Riverhead," Carella said.

"Theodora Franklin of Riverhead," Savage said.

"Yes."

"Well, I've appreciated listening to your ideas."

Carella rose. "None of that was for print, remember," he said.

"Of course not," Savage assured him.

"Thanks for the drink," Carella said.

They shook hands. Savage stayed in the booth and ordered another Tom Collins. Carella went home to shower and shave for his date with Teddy.

* * *

She was dressed resplendently when she opened the door. She stood back, waiting for him to survey her splendor. She was wearing a white linen suit, white straw pumps, a red-stoned pin on the collar of the suit, bright scarlet oval earrings picking up the scream of the pin.

"Shucks," he said, "I was hoping I'd catch you in your slip."

She made a motion to unbutton her jacket, smiling.

"We have reservations," he said.

Where? her face asked.

"Ah Lum Fong," he replied.

She nodded exuberantly.

"Where's your lipstick?" he asked.

She grinned and went to him, and he took her in his arms and kissed her, and then she clung to him as if he were leaving for Siberia in the next ten minutes.

"Come on," he said, "put on your face."

She went into the other room, applied her lipstick and emerged carrying a small red purse.

"They carry those on the Street," he said. "It's a badge of the profession," and she slapped him on the fanny as they left the apartment.

The Chinese restaurant boasted excellent food and an exotic decor. To Carella, the food alone would not have been enough. When he ate in a Chinese restaurant, he wanted it to look and feel Chinese. He did not appreciate an expanded, upholstered version of a Culver Avenue diner.

They ordered fried wonton soup, and lobster

rolls, and barbecued spare ribs and Hon Shu Gai
and Steak Kew and sweet and pungent pork. The
wonton soup was crisp with Chinese vegetables; lus-
cious snow peas, and water chestnuts, and mush-
rooms, and roots he could not have named if he'd
tried. The wontons were brown and crisp, the soup
itself had a rich tangy taste. They talked very little
while they ate. They dug into the lobster rolls, and
then they attacked the spare ribs, succulently
brown.

"Do you know that Lamb thing?" he asked. "A Dis-
sertation on . . ."

She nodded, and then went back to the spare ribs.

The chicken in the Hon Shu Gai was snappingly
crisp. They polished off the dish. They barely had
room for the Steak Kew, but they did their best with
it, and when Charlie—their waiter—came to collect
their dishes, he looked at them reproachfully because they had left over some of the delicious cubes
of beef.

He cut a king pineapple for them in the kitchen,
cut it so that the outside shell could be lifted off in
one piece, exposing the ripe yellow meat beneath
the prickly exterior, the fruit sliced and ready to be
lifted off in long slender pieces. They drank their
tea, savoring the aroma and the warmth, their stom-
achs full, their minds and their bodies relaxed.

"How's August nineteenth sound to you?"

Teddy shrugged.

"It's a Saturday. Would you like to get married on
a Saturday?"

Yes, her eyes said.

Charlie brought them their fortune cookies and replenished the tea pot.

Carella broke open his cookie. Then, before he read the message on the narrow slip of paper, he said, "Do you know the one about the man who opened one of these in a Chinese restaurant?"

Teddy shook her head.

"It said, 'Don't eat the soup. Signed, a friend.' "

Teddy laughed and then gestured to his fortune slip. Carella read it aloud to her:

"You are the luckiest man alive. You are about to marry Theodora Franklin."

She said "Oh!" in soundless exasperation, and then took the slip from him. The slender script read: "You are good with figures."

"Your figure," he said.

Teddy smiled and broke open her cookie. Her face clouded momentarily.

"What is it?" he asked.

She shook her head.

"Let me see it."

She tried to keep the fortune slip from him, but he got it out of her hand and read it.

"Leo will roar—sleep no more."

Carella stared at the printed slip. "That's a hell of a thing to put in a cookie," he said. "What does it mean?" He thought for a moment. "Oh, Leo. Leo the Lion. July 22nd to August something, isn't it?"

Teddy nodded.

"Well, the meaning here is perfectly clear then. Once we're married, you're going to have a hell of a time sleeping."

He grinned, and the worry left her eyes. She smiled, nodded, and then reached across the table for his hand.

The broken cookie rested alongside their hands, and beside that the curled fortune slip.

Leo will roar—sleep no more.

21

The man's name was not Leo.

The man's name was Peter.

His last name was Byrnes.

He was roaring.

"What the hell kind of crap is this, Carella?"

"What?"

"Today's issue of this ... this goddamn rag!" he shouted, pointing to the afternoon tabloid on his desk. "August 4th!"

Leo, Carella thought. "What ... what do you mean, Lieutenant?"

"What do I mean?" Byrnes shouted. "WHAT DO I MEAN? Who the hell gave you the authority to reel off this crap to that idiot Savage?"

"What?"

"There are cops walking beats in Bethtown because they spouted off nonsense like ..."

"Savage? Let me see that ..." Carella started.

Byrnes flipped open the newspaper angrily. "Cop Defies Department!" he shouted. "That's the headline. COP DEFIES DEPARTMENT! What's the matter, Carella, aren't you happy here?"

"Let me see . . ."

"And under that 'MAY KNOW MURDERER,' DETECTIVE SAYS."

"May know . . ."

"Did you tell this to Savage?"

"That I may know who the murderer is? Of course not. Jesus, Pete . . ."

"Don't call me Pete! Here, read the goddamn story."

Carella took the newspaper. For some strange reason, his hands were trembling.

Sure enough, the story was on page four, and it was headlined:

COP DEFIES DEPARTMENT
"MAY KNOW MURDERER,"
DETECTIVE SAYS

"But this is . . ."

"Read it," Byrnes said.

Carella read it.

> *The bar was cool and dim.*
>
> *We sat opposite each other, Detective Stephen Carella and I. He toyed with his drink, and we talked of many things, but mostly we talked of murder.*
>
> *"I've got an idea I know who killed those three cops," Carella said. "It's not the kind of idea you can take to your superiors, though. They wouldn't understand."*

And so came the first ray of hope in the mystery which has baffled the mastermods of Homicide North and tied the hands of stubborn, opinionated Detective-Lieutenant Peter Byrnes of the 87th Precinct.

"I can't tell you very much more about it right now," Carella said, "because I'm still digging. But this cop-hater theory is all wrong. It's something in the personal lives of these three men, of that I'm sure. It needs work, but we'll crack it."

So spoke Detective Carella yesterday afternoon in a bar in the heart of the Murder Belt. He is a shy, withdrawn man, a man who—in his own words—is "not seeking glory."

"Police work is like any other kind of work," he told me, "except that we deal in crime. When you've got a hunch, you dig into it. If it pans out, then you bring it to your superiors, and maybe they'll listen, and maybe they won't."

Thus far, he has confided his "hunch" only to his fiancée, a lovely young lady named Theodora Franklin, a girl from Riverhead. Miss Franklin feels that Carella can "do no wrong," and is certain he will crack the case despite the inadequate fumblings of the department to date.

"There are skeletons in the closets," Carella said. "And those skeletons point to our man. We've got to dig deeper. It's just a matter of time now."

We sat in the cool dimness of the bar, and I felt the quiet strength emanating from this man who has the courage to go ahead with his investigation in spite of the Cop-Hater Theory which pervades the dusty minds of the men working around him.

This man will find the murderer, I thought.

This man will relieve the city of its constant fear, its dread of an unknown killer roaming the streets with a wanton .45 automatic in his blood-stained fist. This man . . .

"Jesus!" Carella said.

"Yeah," Byrnes answered. "Now what about it?"

"I never said these things. I mean, not this way. And he said it wasn't for print!" Carella suddenly exploded. "Where's the phone? I'm going to sue this son of a bitch for libel! He can't get away with . . ."

"Calm down," Byrnes said.

"Why'd he drag Teddy into this? Does he want to make her a sitting duck for that stupid bastard with the .45? Is he out of his mind?"

"Calm down," Byrnes repeated.

"Calm down? I never said I knew who the murderer was! I never . . ."

"What did you say?"

"I only said I had an idea that I wanted to work on."

"And what's the idea?"

"That maybe this guy wasn't after cops at all. Maybe he was just after men. And maybe not even that. Maybe he was just after *one* man."

"Which one?"

"How the hell do I know? Why'd he mention Teddy? Jesus, what's the matter with this guy?"

"Nothing that a head doctor couldn't cure," Byrnes said.

"Listen, I want to go up to see Teddy. God knows . . ."

"What time is it?" Byrnes asked.

Carella looked at the wall clock. "Six-fifteen."

"Wait until six-thirty. Havilland will be back from supper by then."

"If I ever meet this guy Savage again," Carella promised, "I'm going to rip him in half."

"Or at least give him a speeding ticket," Byrnes commented.

The man in the black suit stood outside the apartment door, listening. A copy of the afternoon newspaper stuck up from the right-hand pocket of his jacket. His left shoulder throbbed with pain, and the weight of the .45 automatic tugged at the other pocket of his jacket, so that—favoring the wound, bearing the weight of the gun—he leaned slightly to his left while he listened.

There was no sound from within the apartment.

He had read the name very carefully in the newspaper, Theodora Franklin, and then he had checked the Riverhead directory and come up with the address. He wanted to talk to this girl. He wanted to find out how much Carella knew. He had to find out.

She's very quiet in there, he thought. *What's she doing?*

Cautiously, he tried the doorknob. He wiggled it slowly from side to side. The door was locked.

He heard footsteps. He tried to back away from the door too late. He reached for the gun in his pocket. The door was opening, wide, wider.

The girl stood there, surprised. She was a pretty girl, small, dark-haired, wide brown eyes. She wore a white chenille robe. The robe was damp in spots. He assumed she had just come from the shower. Her eyes went to his face, and then to the gun in his hand. Her mouth opened, but no sound came from it. She tried to slam the door, but he rammed his foot into the wedge and then shoved it back.

She moved away from him, deeper into the room. He closed the door and locked it.

"Miss Franklin?" he asked.

She nodded, terrified. She had seen the drawing on the front pages of all the newspapers, had seen it broadcast on all the television programs. There was no mistake, this was the man Steve was looking for.

"Let's have a little talk, shall we?" he asked.

His voice was a nice voice, smooth, almost suave. He was a good-looking man, why had he killed those cops? Why would a man like this . . . ?

"Did you hear me?" he asked.

She nodded. She could read his lips, could understand everything he said, but . . .

"What does your boyfriend know?" he asked.

He held the .45 loosely, as if he were accustomed to its lethal power now, as if he considered it a toy more than a dangerous weapon.

"What's the matter, you scared?"

She touched her hands to her lips, pulled them away in a gesture of futility.

"What?"

She repeated the gesture.

"Come on," he said, "talk, for Christ's sake! You're not that scared!"

Again, she repeated the gesture, shook her head this time. He watched her curiously.

"I'll be damned," he said at last. "A dummy!" He began laughing. The laugh filled the apartment, reverberating from the walls. "A dummy! If that don't take the cake! A dummy!" His laughter died. He studied her carefully. "You're not trying to pull something, are you?"

She shook her head vigorously. Her hands went to the opening of her robe, clutching the chenille to her more tightly.

"Now this has definite advantages, doesn't it?" he said, grinning. "You can't scream, you can't use the phone, you can't do a damned thing, can you?"

Teddy swallowed, watching him.

"What does Carella know?" he asked.

She shook her head.

"The paper said he's got a lead. Does he know about me? Does he have any idea who I am?"

Again, she shook her head.

"I don't believe you."

She nodded, trying to convince him that Steve

knew nothing. What paper was he referring to? What did he mean? She spread her hands wide, indicating innocence, hoping he would understand.

He reached into his jacket pocket and tossed the newspaper to her.

"Page four," he said. "Read it. I've got to sit down. This goddamn shoulder . . ."

He sat, the gun leveled at her. She opened the paper and read the story, shaking her head as she read.

"Well?" he asked.

She kept shaking her head. *No, this is not true. No, Steve would never say things like these. Steve would . . .*

"What'd he tell you?" the man asked.

Her eyes opened wide with pleading. *Nothing, he told me nothing.*

"The newspaper says . . ."

She hurled the paper to the floor.

"Lies, huh?"

Yes, she nodded.

His eyes narrowed. "Newspapers don't lie," he said.

They do, they do!

"When's he coming here?"

She stood motionless, controlling her face, not wanting her face to betray anything to the man with the gun.

"Is he coming?"

She shook her head.

"You're lying. It's all over your face. He's coming here, isn't he?"

She bolted for the door. He caught her arm and

flung her back across the room. The robe pulled back over her legs when she fell to the floor. She pulled it together quickly and stared up at him.

"Don't try that again," he said.

Her breath came heavily now. She sensed a coiled spring within this man, a spring which would unleash itself at the door the moment Steve opened it. But he'd said he would not be there until midnight. He had told her that, and there were a lot of hours between now and midnight. In that time . . .

"You just get out of the shower?" he asked.

She nodded.

"Those are good legs," he said, and she felt his eyes on her. "Dames," he said philosophically. "What've you got on under that robe?"

Her eyes widened.

He began laughing. "Just what I thought. Smart. Good way to beat the heat. When's Carella coming?"

She did not answer.

"Seven, eight, nine? Is he on duty today?" He watched her. "Nothing from you, huh? What's he got, the four to midnight? Sure, otherwise he'd probably be with you right this minute. Well, we might as well make ourselves comfortable, we got a long wait. Anything to drink in this place?"

Teddy nodded.

"What've you got? Gin? Rye? Bourbon?" He watched her. "Gin? You got tonic? No, huh? Club soda? Okay, mix me a Collins. Hey, where you going?"

Teddy gestured to the kitchen.

"I'll come with you," he said. He followed her into

the kitchen. She opened the refrigerator and took out an opened bottle of club soda.

"Haven't you got a fresh one?" he asked. Her back was to him, and so she could not read his lips. He seized her shoulder and swung her around. His hand did not leave her shoulder.

"I asked you if you had a fresh bottle," he said.

She nodded and bent, taking an unopened bottle from the lowest shelf of the refrigerator. She took lemons from the fruit drawer, and then went to the cupboard for the bottle of gin.

"Dames," he said again.

She poured a double shot of gin into a tall glass. She spooned sugar into the glass, and then she went to one of the drawers.

"Hey!"

He saw the knife in her hand.

"Don't get ideas with that. Just slice the lemon."

She sliced the lemon and squeezed both halves into the glass. She poured club soda until the glass was three-quarters full, and then she went back to the refrigerator for the ice cubes. When the drink was finished, she handed it to him.

"Make one for yourself," he said.

She shook her head.

"I said make one for yourself! I don't like to drink alone."

Patiently, wearily, she made herself a drink.

"Come on. Back in the living room."

They went into the living room, and he sat in an easy chair, wincing as he adjusted himself so that his shoulder was comfortable.

"When the knock comes on the door," he said, "you just sit tight, understand? Go unlock it now."

She went to the door and unlocked it. And now, knowing that the door was open, knowing that Steve would enter and be faced with a blazing .45, she felt fear crawl into her head like a nest of spiders.

"What are you thinking?" he asked.

She shrugged. She walked back into the room and sat opposite him, facing the door.

"This is a good drink," he said. "Come on, drink."

She sipped at the Collins, her mind working ahead to the moment of Steve's arrival.

"I'm going to kill him, you know," he said.

She watched him, her eyes wide.

"Won't make any difference now, anyway, will it? One cop more or less. Make it look a little better, don't you think?"

She was puzzled, and the puzzlement showed on her face.

"It's the best way," he explained. "If he knows something, well, it won't do to have him around. And if he doesn't know anything, it'll round out the picture." He struggled in the chair. "Jesus, I've got to get this shoulder fixed. How'd you like that lousy doctor? That was something, wasn't it? I thought they were supposed to be healers."

He talks the way anyone does, she thought. *Except that he talks so casually of death. He is going to kill Steve.*

"We were figuring on Mexico, anyway. Going to leave this afternoon, until your boyfriend came up with his bright idea. We'll take off in the morning, though. Soon as I take care of this." He paused. "Do you suppose I can get a good doctor in Mexico? Jesus, the things a guy will do, huh?" He watched her face carefully. "You ever been in love?"

She studied him, puzzled, confused. He did not seem like a killer. She nodded.

"Who with? This cop?"

She nodded again.

"Well, that's a shame." He seemed sincerely sorry. "It's a damn shame, honey, but what hasta be hasta be. There's no other way, you can see that, can't you? I mean, there was no other way right from the start, from the minute I started this thing. And when you start something, you've got to see it through right to the finish. It's a matter of survival now, you realize that? Jesus, the things a guy will do. Well, you know." He paused. "You'd kill for him, wouldn't you?"

She hesitated.

"To keep him, you'd kill for him, wouldn't you?" he repeated.

She nodded.

"So? So there." He smiled. "I'm not a professional, you know. I'm a mechanic. That's my line. I'm a damn good mechanic, too. Think I'll be able to get work in Mexico?"

Teddy shrugged.

"Sure, they must have cars down there. They've got cars everywhere. Then, later, when things have cooled down, we'll come back to the States. Hell, things should cool down sooner or later. But what I'm trying to tell you, I'm not a professional killer, so don't get that idea. I'm just a regular guy."

Her eyes did not believe him.

"No, huh? Well, I'm telling you. Sometimes, there's no other way out. If you see something's hopeless, and somebody explains to you where there's some hope, okay, you take it. I never harmed nobody until I killed those cops. You think I wanted to kill them? Survival, that's all. Some things, you've got to do. Agh, what the hell do you understand? You're just a dummy."

She sat silent, watching him.

"A woman gets under your skin. Some women are like that. Listen, I've been around. I've been around plenty. I had me more dames than you could count. But this one—different. Different right from the beginning. She just got under my skin. Right under it. When it gets you like that, you can't eat, you can't sleep, nothing. You just think about her all day long. And what can you do when you realize you can't really have her unless . . . well . . . unless you . . . hell, didn't she ask him for a divorce? Is it my fault he was a stubborn son of a bitch? Well, he's still stubborn— only now he's dead."

Teddy's eyes moved from his face. They covered the door behind him, and then dropped to the doorknob.

"And he took two of his pals with him." He stared into his glass. "Those are the breaks. He should've listened to reason. A woman like her . . . Jesus, you'd do anything for a woman like her. Anything! Just being in the same room with her, you want to . . ."

Teddy watched the knob with fascination. She rose suddenly. She brought back her glass and then threw it at him. It grazed his forehead, the liquid splashing out of the glass and cascading over his shoulder. He leaped to his feet, his face twisted in fury, the .45 pointed at her.

"You stupid bitch!" he bellowed. "Why the hell did you do that?"

22

Carella left the precinct at 6:30 on the button. Havilland had not yet come back from supper, but he could wait no longer. He did not want to leave Teddy alone in that apartment, not after the fool stunt Savage had pulled.

He drove to Riverhead quickly. He ignored traffic lights and full stop signs. He ignored everything. There was an all-consuming thought in his mind, and that thought included a man with a .45 and a girl with no tongue.

When he reached her apartment building, he glanced up at her window. The shades were not drawn. The apartment looked very quiet. He breathed a little more easily, and then entered the building. He climbed the steps, his heart pounding. He knew he shouldn't be alarmed but he could not shake the persistent feeling that Savage's column had invited danger for Teddy.

He stopped outside her door. He could hear the persistent drone of what sounded like the radio going inside. He reached for the knob. In his usual manner, he twisted it slowly from side to side, waiting for her footsteps, knowing she would come to the door the moment she saw his signal.

He heard the sound of a chair scraping back and then someone shouted, "You stupid bitch! Why the hell did you do that?"

His brain came alive. He reached for his .38 and snapped the door open with his other hand.

The man turned.

"You . . . !" he shouted, and the .45 bucked in his hand.

Carella fired low, dropping to the floor the instant he entered the room. His first two shots took the man in the thigh. The man fell face forward, the .45 pitching out of his fist. Carella kicked back the hammer on the .38, waiting.

"You bastard," the man on the floor said. "You bastard."

Carella got to his feet. He picked up the .45 and stuck it into his back pocket.

"Get up," he said. "You all right, Teddy?"

Teddy nodded. She was breathing heavily, watching the man on the floor.

"Thanks for the warning," Carella said. He turned to the man again. "Get up!"

"I can't, you bastard. Why'd you shoot me? For Christ's sake, why'd you shoot me?"

"Why'd you shoot three cops?"

The man went silent.

"What's your name?" Carella asked.

"Mercer. Paul Mercer."

"Don't you like cops?"

"I love them."

"What's the story then?"

"I suppose you're going to check my gun with what you've already got."

"Damn right," Carella said. "You haven't got a chance, Mercer."

"She put me up to it," Mercer said, a scowl on his dark face. "She's the real murderer. All I done was pull the trigger. She said we had to kill him, said it was the only way. We threw the others in just to make it look good, just to make it look as if a cop hater was loose. But it was her idea. Why should I take the rap alone?"

"Whose idea?" Carella asked.

"Alice's," Mercer said. "You see . . . we wanted to make it look like a cop hater. We wanted . . ."

"It was," Carella said.

When they brought Alice Bush in, she was dressed in grey, a quiet grey. She sat in the squad room, crossing her legs.

"Do you have a cigarette, Steve?" she asked.

Carella gave her one. He did not light it for her. She sat with the cigarette dangling from her lips until it was apparent she would have to light it herself. Unruffled, she struck a match.

"What about it?" Carella asked.

"What about it?" she repeated, shrugging. "It's all over, isn't it?"

"You must have really hated him. You must have hated him like poison."

"You're directing," Alice said. "I'm only the star."

"Don't get glib, Alice!" Carella said angrily. "I've never hit a woman in my life, but I swear to God . . ."

"Relax," she told him. "It's all over. You'll get your gold star, and then you'll . . ."

"Alice . . ."

"What the hell do you want me to do? Break down and cry? I hated him, all right? I hated his big, pawing hands and I hated his stupid red hair, and I hated everything about him, all right?"

"Mercer said you'd asked for a divorce. Is that true?"

"No, I didn't ask for a divorce. Hank would've never agreed to one."

"Why didn't you give him a chance?"

"What for? Did he ever give me a chance? Cooped up in that goddamn apartment, waiting for him to come off some burglary or some knifing or some mugging? What kind of life is that for a woman?"

"You knew he was a cop when you married him."

Alice didn't answer.

"You could've asked for a divorce, Alice. You could've tried."

"I didn't want to, damnit. *I wanted him dead.*"

"Well, you've got him dead. Him and two others. You must be tickled now."

Alice smiled suddenly. "I'm not too worried, Steve."

"No?"

"There have to be *some* men on the jury." She paused. "Men like me."

* * *

There were, in fact, eight men on the jury.

The jury brought in a verdict in six minutes flat.

Mercer was sobbing as the jury foreman read off the verdict and the judge gave sentence. Alice listened to the judge with calm indifference, her shoulders thrown back, her head erect.

The jury had found them both guilty of murder in the first degree, and the judge sentenced them to death in the electric chair.

On August nineteenth, Stephen Carella and Theodora Franklin listened to their own sentence.

"Do either of you know of any reason why you both should not be legally joined in marriage, or if there be any present who can show any just cause why these parties should not be legally joined together, let him now speak or hereafter hold his peace."

Lieutenant Byrnes held his peace. Detective Hal Willis said nothing. The small gathering of friends and relatives watched, dewy-eyed.

The city clerk turned to Carella.

"Do you, Stephen Louis Carella, take this woman as your lawfully wedded wife to live together in the state of matrimony? Will you love, honor and keep her as a faithful man is bound to do, in health, sickness, prosperity and adversity, and forsaking all others keep you alone unto her as long as you both shall live?"

"Yes," Carella said. "Yes, I will. I do. Yes."

"Do you, Theodora Franklin, take this man as your lawfully wedded husband to live together in the state of matrimony? Will you love, honor and cherish him as a faithful woman is bound to do, in health, sickness, prosperity and adversity, and forsaking all others keep you alone unto him as long as you both shall live?"

Teddy nodded. There were tears in her eyes, but she could not keep the ecstatic smile off her face.

"For as you both have consented in wedlock and have acknowledged it before this company, I do by virtue of the authority vested in me by the laws of this state now pronounce you husband and wife. And may God bless your union."

Carella took her in his arms and kissed her. The clerk smiled. Lieutenant Byrnes cleared his throat. Willis looked up at the ceiling. The clerk kissed Teddy when Carella released her. Byrnes kissed her. Willis kissed her. All the male relatives and friends came up to kiss her.

Carella smiled idiotically.

"You hurry back," Byrnes said to him.

"Hurry back? I'm going on my honeymoon, Pete!"

"Well, hurry anyway. How are we going to run that precinct without you? You're the only cop in the city who has the courage to buck the decisions of stubborn, opinionated Detective-Lieutenant Byrnes of the . . ."

"Oh, go to hell," Carella said, smiling.

Willis shook his hand. "Good luck, Steve. She's a wonderful gal."

"Thank you, Hal."

Teddy came to him. He put his arm around her.

"Well," he said, "let's go."

They went out of the room together.

Byrnes stared after them wistfully.

"He's a good cop," he said.

"Yeah," Willis answered.

"Come on," Byrnes said, "let's go see what's brew-ing back at the house."

They went down into the street together.

"Want to get a paper," Byrnes said. He stopped at a newsstand and picked up a copy of Savage's tabloid. The trial news had been crowded right off the front pages. There was more important news. The headlines simply read:

HEAT WAVE BREAKS!
HAPPY DAY!

We interrogate the "Grand Master of American Mystery," ED McBAIN

ON WRITING AN 87th PRECINCT NOVEL:

"I usually start with a corpse.
I then ask myself how the corpse
got to be that way and I try to
find out—just as the cops would.
I plot, loosely, usually a chapter
or two ahead, going back to make sure
that everything fits—all the clues are
in the right places, all the bodies are
accounted for... [I] believe strongly in the
long arm of coincidence because I know cops
well, I know how much it contributes
to the solving of real police cases."

2348

ON VIOLENCE IN HIS NOVELS:

"I am unflinching about the violence...If someone is getting killed, that person is getting killed and you know it, and it hurts, and it results in a torn body lying on the sidewalk. It's not pretty...it's horrible. But there's a way of doing violence that's salacious. And that's wrong...I have never, ever, ever in my books tried to make violence appealing. I've made it frightening and I've made it ugly, but never appealing."

ON POLICE REACTION TO 87th PRECINCT NOVELS:

"I get a lot of mail from cops pleased with the accuracy of my books, and if I ever need any help with any problems that may crop up while working on a book, I know who to turn to. After all, some of my best friends are cops."

ON WHAT HIS 87th PRECINCT NOVELS ARE ALL ABOUT:

"I think of the 87th as one big book, a changing portrait of a big city and of crime and punishment in our time."

The fiction of Ed McBain
Published by Pocket Books

2349

POCKET BOOKS
PROUDLY PRESENTS

The Last Dance
A Novel of the 87th Precinct

Ed McBain

Coming soon in hardcover
from Simon & Schuster

The following is a preview of
The Last Dance. . . .

1

"He had heart trouble," the woman was telling Carella.

Which perhaps accounted for the tiny pinpricks of blood on the dead man's eyeballs. In cases of acute right-heart failure, you often found such hemorrhaging. The grayish-blue feet sticking out from under the edge of the blanket were another matter.

"Told me he hadn't been feeling good these past few days," the woman was saying. "I kept telling him to go see the doctor. Yeah, I'll go, I'll go, don't worry, like that, you know? So I stopped by this morning to see how he was, found him just this way. In bed. Dead."

"So you called the police." Meyer said, nodding.

Because he'd expected to go out on a narcotics plant this morning, he was wearing blue jeans, a sweat shirt, and Reeboks. Instead, he'd caught this one with Carella and here he was. On a fishing expedition with a woman he felt was lying. Burly and bald, he posed his question with wide, blue-eyed innocence, just as if it did not conceal a hand grenade.

"Yes," she said, "I called the police. That was the first thing I did."

"Knew straight off he was dead, is that right?"

"Well . . . yes. I could see he was dead."

"You didn't take his pulse or anything like that, did you?" Carella asked.

Looking trimmer and fitter than he had in a long while—he had deliberately lost six pounds since his fortieth birthday—he was dressed casually this morning in dark blue trousers, a gray corduroy jacket, a plaid sports shirt, and a dark blue knit tie. He had not anticipated this particular squeal at a little past ten in the morning. In fact, he had scheduled a ten-fifteen squadroom interview with a burglary victim. Instead, here he was, talking to a woman he too felt was lying.

"No," she said. "Well, yes. Well, not his pulse. But I leaned over him. To see if he was still breathing. But I could see he was dead. I mean . . . well, look at him."

The dead man was lying on his back, covered with a blanket, his eyes and mouth open, his tongue protruding. Carella glanced at him again, a faint look of sorrow and pain momentarily knifing his eyes. In these moments, he felt particularly vulnerable, wondering as he often did if he was perhaps unsuited to a job that brought him into frequent contact with death.

"So you called the police," Meyer said again.

"Yes. Told whoever answered the phone . . ."

"Was this 911 you called? Or the precinct number direct?"

"911. I don't know the precinct number. I don't live around here."

"Told the operator you'd come into your father's apartment and found him dead, is that right?"

"Yes."

"What time was this, Miss?"

"A little after ten this morning. It's Mrs., by the way," she said almost apologetically.

Carella looked at his watch. It was now twenty minutes to eleven. He wondered where the medical examiner was. Couldn't touch anything in here till the M.E. pronounced the victim dead. He wanted to see the rest of the body. Wanted to see if the legs matched the feet.

"Mrs. Robert Keating," the woman said. "Well, *Cynthia* Keating, actually."

"And your father's name?"

"Andrew. Andrew Hale."

Better to let Meyer stay with it for now, Carella thought. He had noticed the same things Carella had, was equally familiar with the telltale signs of a hanging, which this one resembled a great deal, but you couldn't hang yourself lying flat on your back in bed with no noose around your neck.

"How old was he, can you tell us?"

"Sixty-eight."

"And you say he had heart trouble?"

"Two heart attacks in the past eight years."

"Serious?"

"Oh yes."

"Bypasses?"

"No. Two angioplasties. But his condition was very grave. He almost lost his life each time."

"And he continued having trouble, is that it?"

"Well . . . no."

"You said he had heart trouble."

"Two serious heart attacks in eight years, yes, that's heart trouble. But he wasn't restricted in his activities or anything."

"Good morning, gentlemen," a voice said from the bedroom doorway. For a moment, the detectives couldn't tell whether the man standing there was Carl Blaney or Paul Blaney. Not very many people knew that Carl Blaney and Paul Blaney were twin brothers. Most of the detectives in this city had spoken to them separately, either on the phone or in person at the morgue, but they assumed the similarity of their surnames and the fact that they both worked for the Medical Examiner's Office were attributable to mere coincidence. As every working cop knew, coincidence was a major factor in police work.

Both Blaneys were five feet, nine inches tall. Paul Blaney weighed a hundred and eighty pounds, whereas his brother Carl weighed a hundred and sixty-five. Carl still had all of his hair. Paul was going a bit bald at the back of his head. Both Paul and Carl had violet eyes, although neither was related to Elizabeth Taylor.

"Carl," the man in the doorway said, clearing up any confusion at once. He was wearing a lightweight topcoat, a plaid muffler draped loose around his neck. He took off the coat and muffler and threw them over a straight-backed chair just inside the bedroom door.

"You are?" he asked Cynthia.

"His daughter," she said.

"I'm sorry for your trouble," he told her, managing to sound as if he actually meant it. "I'd like to examine your father now," he said. "Would you mind stepping outside, please?"

"Yes, of course," she said, and started for the doorway, and then stopped, and asked, "Shall I call my husband?"

"Might be a good idea," Carella said.

"He works nearby," she said to no one in particular and then went out into the kitchen. They could hear her dialing the wall phone there.

"What's it look like?" Blaney asked.

"Asphyxia," Carella said.

Blaney was already at the bed, leaning over the dead man as if about to kiss him on the lips. He noticed the eyes at once. "This what you mean?" he asked. "The petechiae?"

"Yes."

"By no means conclusive evidence of death by asphyxia," Blaney said flatly. "You should know that, Detective. This how he was found? On his back this way?"

"According to the daughter."

"Couldn't have accidentally smothered then, could he?"

"I guess not."

"You have any reason to disbelieve her?"

"Just the blood spots. And the blue feet."

"Oh? Do we have blue feet as well?" Blaney asked, and looked toward the foot of the bed. "Are we suspecting death by hanging then? Is that it?"

"The daughter says he had a history of heart disease," Carella said. "Maybe it was heart failure. Who knows?"

"Who knows indeed?" Blaney asked the dead man's feet. "Let's see what else we've got here, shall we?" he said, and threw back the blanket.

The dead man was wearing a white shirt open at the throat, gray flannel trousers fastened with a black belt. No shoes or socks.

"Goes to bed with all his clothes on, I see," Blaney said dryly.

"Barefoot though," Carella said.

Blaney grunted, unbuttoned the shirt, and slid a stethoscope onto the dead man's chest, not expecting to find a heartbeat, and not surprised when he didn't. He removed all the man's garments—he was also wearing striped boxer shorts—and noticed at once the grayish-blue coloration of the corpse's legs, forearms, and hands. "*If* he was hanged," he told Carella, "and I'm not saying he was, then it was in an upright position. And *if* he was moved to the bed here, and I'm not saying he was, then it wasn't too soon after he died. Otherwise the postmortem lividity would have faded from the extremities and moved to the back and buttocks. Let's take a look," he said and rolled the dead man onto his side. His back was pale, his ass as white as a full moon. "Nope," he said, and rolled the corpse onto his back again. The man's penis was swollen and distended. "Postmortem lividity," Blaney explained. "Settling of tissue fluids." There were dried stains in the corpse's undershorts. "Probably semen," Blaney said. "We don't know why, but a seminal discharge is commonplace in cases of asphyxia. Has nothing to do with any sexual activity. Rigor mortis in the seminal vesicles causes it." He looked at Carella. Carella merely nodded. "No rope burns," Blaney said, examining the neck, "no imprint of a noose, no blisters from pinching or squeezing of the skin. A knot may have caused this," he said, indicating a small bruise under the chin. "Did you find any kind of noose?"

"We haven't really made a search yet," Carella said.

"Well, it certainly *looks* like a hanging," Blaney said, "but who knows?"

"Who knows indeed?" Carella echoed, as if they were going through a familiar vaudeville routine.

"If I were you, I'd talk to the daughter some more," Blaney said. "Let's see what the autopsy shows. Meanwhile, he's dead and he's yours."

The mobile crime unit arrived some ten minutes later, after the body and Blaney were both gone. Carella told them to keep a special lookout for fibers. The chief technician told him they were *always* on the lookout for fibers, what did he mean by a *special* lookout? Carella cut his eyes toward where Meyer was talking to Cynthia Keating across the room. The chief technician still didn't know why a special lookout for fibers was necessary, but he didn't ask Carella anything else.

It was starting to rain.

The mandatory date for turning on the heat in this city was October fifteenth—birthdate of great men, Carella thought, but did not say. This was already the twenty-ninth but too many buildings took their time complying with the law. The rain and the falling temperature outside combined to make it a little chilly in the apartment. The technicians, who had just come in from the cold, kept their coats on. Carella put his coat back on before ambling over to where Meyer was idly and casually chatting up the dead man's daughter. They both wanted to know if she'd found the body exactly where she said she'd found it, but they weren't asking that just yet.

". . . or did you just drop by?" Meyer said.

"He knew I was coming."

"Did he know what time?"

"No. I just said I'd be by sometime this morning."

"But he was still in bed when you got here?"

The key question.

"Yes," she said.

No hesitation on her part.

"Wearing all his clothes?" Carella asked.

She turned toward him. Bad Cop flashed in her eyes. Too many damn television shows these days, everyone knew all the cop tricks.

"Yes," she said. "Well, not his shoes and socks."

"Did he always sleep with his clothes on?" Carella asked.

"No. He must have gotten up and . . ."

"Yes?" Meyer said.

She turned to look at him, suspecting Good Cop, but not yet certain.

"Gone back to bed again," she explained.

"I see," Meyer said, and turned to Carella as if seeking approval of this perfectly reasonable explanation of why a man was in bed with all his clothes on except for his shoes and socks.

"Maybe he felt something coming on," Cynthia said further.

"Something coming on?" Meyer said, encouraging her.

"Yes. A heart attack. People know when they're coming."

"I see. And you figure he might have gone to lie down."

"Yes."

"Didn't call an ambulance or anything," Carella said. "Just went to lie down."

"Yes. Thinking it might pass. The heart attack."

"Took off his shoes and socks and went to lie down."

"Yes."

"Was the door locked when you got here?" Carella asked.

"I have a key."

"Then it was locked."

"Yes."

"Did you knock?"

"I knocked, but there was no answer. So I let myself in."

"And found your father in bed."

"Yes."

"Were his shoes and socks where they are now?"

"Yes."

"On the floor there? Near the easy chair?"

"Yes."

"So you called the police." Meyer said for the third time.

"Yes," Cynthia said, and looked at him.

"Did you suspect foul play of any sort?" Carella asked.

"No. Of course not."

"But you called the police," Meyer said.

"Why is that important?" she snapped, suddenly tipping to what was going on here, Good Cop becoming Bad Cop in the wink of an eye.

"He's merely asking," Carella said.

"No, he's not merely asking, he seems to think it's important. He keeps asking me over and over again did I call the police, did I call the police, when you *know* I called the police, otherwise you wouldn't *be* here!"

"We have to ask certain questions," Carella said gently.

"But why that particular question?"

"Because some people wouldn't necessarily call the police if they found someone dead from apparent natural causes."

"Who would they call? Necessarily?"

"Relatives, friends, even a lawyer. Not necessarily

the police, is all my partner's saying," Carella explained gently.

"Then why doesn't he *say* it?" Cynthia snapped. "Instead of asking me all the time did I call the *police?*"

"I'm sorry, ma'am," Meyer said in his most abject voice. "I didn't mean to suggest there was anything peculiar about your calling the police."

"Well, your *partner* here seems to think it was peculiar," Cynthia said, thoroughly confused now. "*He* seems to think I should have called my husband or my girlfriend or my priest or anybody *but* the police, what *is* it with you two?"

"We simply have to investigate every possibility," Carella said, more convinced than ever that she was lying. "By all appearances, your father died in bed, possibly from a heart attack, possibly from some other cause, we won't know that until the autopsy results are . . . "

"He was an old man who'd suffered two previous heart attacks," Cynthia said. "What do you *think* he died of?"

"I don't know, ma'am," Carella said. "Do you?"

Cynthia looked him dead in the eye.

"My husband's a lawyer, you know," she said.

"Is your mother still alive?" Meyer asked, ducking the question and its implied threat.

"He's on the way here now," she said, not turning to look at Meyer, her gaze still fastened on Carella as if willing him to melt under her very eyes. Green, he noticed. A person could easily melt under a green-eyed laser beam.

"Is she?" Meyer asked.

"She's alive," Cynthia said. "But they're divorced."

"Any other children besides you?"

She glared at Carella a moment longer, and then

turned to Meyer, seemingly calmer now. "Just me," she said.

"How long have they been divorced?" Meyer asked.

"Five years."

"What was his current situation?"

"What do you mean?"

"Your father. Was he living with anyone?"

"I have no idea."

"Seeing anyone?"

"His private life was his own business."

"How often did you see your father, Mrs. Keating?"

"Around once a month."

"Had he been complaining about his heart lately?" Carella asked.

"Not to me, no. But you know how old men are. They don't take care of themselves."

"Was he complaining about his heart to anyone at *all*?" Meyer asked.

"Not that I know of."

"Then what makes you think he died of a heart attack?" Carella asked.

Cynthia looked first at him, and then at Meyer, and then at Carella again.

"I don't think I like either one of you," she said, and walked out into the kitchen to stand alone by the window.

One of the technicians had been hovering. He caught Carella's eye now. Carella nodded and went over to him.

"Blue cashmere belt," the technician said. "Blue cashmere fibers over the door hook there. What do you think?"

"Where's the belt?"

"Near the chair there," he said, and indicated the easy chair near the room's single dresser. A blue bathrobe was draped over the back of the chair. The belt to the robe was on the floor, alongside the dead man's shoes and socks.

"And the hook?"

"Back of the bathroom door."

Carella glanced across the room. The bathroom door was open. A chrome hook was screwed into the door, close to the top.

"The robe has loops for the belt," the technician said. "Seems funny it's loose on the floor."

"They fall off all the time," Carella said.

"Sure, I know. But it ain't every day we get a guy dead in bed who looks like maybe he was hanged."

"How strong is that hook?"

"It doesn't have to be," the technician said. "All a hanging does is interrupt the flow of blood to the brain. That can be done by the weight of the head alone. We're talking an average of ten pounds. A *picture* hook can support that."

"You should take the detective's exam," Carella suggested, smiling.

"Thanks, but I'm already Second Grade," the technician said. "Point is, the belt coulda been knotted around the old man's neck and then thrown over the hook to hang him. That's if the fibers match."

"And provided he didn't customarily hang his robe over that hook."

"You looking for a hundred excuses to prove he died of natural causes? Or you looking for one that says it could've been homicide?"

"Who said anything about homicide?"

"Gee, excuse me, I thought that's what you were looking for, Detective."

"How about a suicide made to look like natural causes?"

"That'd be a good one," the technician agreed.

"When will you have the test results?"

"Late this afternoon sometime?"

"I'll call you."

"My card," the technician said.

"Detective?" a man's voice said.

Carella turned toward the kitchen doorway where a burly man in a dark gray coat with a black velvet collar was standing. The shoulders of the coat were damp with rain, and his face was raw and red from the cold outside. He wore a little mustache under his nose, and he had puffy cheeks, and very dark brown eyes.

"I'm Robert Keating," he said, walking toward Carella, but not extending his hand in greeting. His wife stood just behind him. They had obviously talked since he'd come into the apartment. There was an anticipatory look on her face, as if she expected her husband to punch one of the detectives. Carella certainly hoped he wouldn't.

"I understand you've been hassling my wife," Keating said.

"I wasn't aware of that, sir," Carella said.

"I'm here to tell you that better not be the case."

Carella was thinking it better not be the case that your wife came in here and found her father hanging from the bathroom door and took him down and carried him to the bed. That had better not be the case here.

"I'm sorry if there was any misunderstanding, sir," he said.

"There had better *not* be any misunderstanding," Keating said.

"Just so there won't be," Carella said, "let me make our intentions clear. If your father-in-law died of a heart attack, you can bury him in the morning, and you'll never see us again as long as you live. But if he died for some other reason, then we'll be trying to find out why, and you're liable to see us around for quite a while. Okay, sir?"

"This is a crime scene, sir," the technician said. "Want to clear the premises, please?"

"What?" Keating said.

At four-thirty that afternoon, Carella called the lab downtown and asked to talk to Detective Second Grade Anthony Moreno. Moreno got on the phone and told him the fibers they'd lifted from the hook on the bathroom door positively matched sample fibers from the robe's blue cashmere belt.

Not ten minutes later, Carl Blaney called Carella to tell him that the autopsy findings in the death of Andrew Henry Hale were consistent with post-mortem appearances in asphyxial deaths.

Carella wondered if Cynthia Keating's husband would accompany her to the squadroom when they asked her to come in.

Look for
THE LAST DANCE
Wherever Books
Are Sold.
Coming Soon from
Simon & Schuster.